POWER
in
MANAGEMENT

POWER
in
MANAGEMENT

John P. Kotter

amacom
A Division of American Management Associations

Library of Congress Cataloging in Publication Data

Kotter, John P   1947-
  Power in management.

  Includes index.
  1. Management.   2. Power (Social science)
I. Title.
HD38.K64   658.4   78-31558
ISBN 0-8144-5507-7

© 1979 AMACOM
A division of American Management Associations, New York.
All rights reserved. Printed in the United States of America.

Third Printing

Acknowledgments

The concepts and examples in this book come from a variety of sources. Most of the material has evolved from my experiences in an investigation conducted during 1974 and 1975. In this effort, 26 different organizations were studied and well over 200 managers were interviewed. All names of people and organizations given as examples have been disguised. The organizations in this study included:

Financial Institutions (a small bank, a large trust company, a medium-size insurance company, and a small money management firm)

Business Services (a large consulting firm, a medium-size consulting firm, and a large advertising agency)

Manufacturers (a small jewelry company, a moderate-size shoe manufacturer, a small candy company, a small scientific instruments company, and two Fortune 500 corporations)

Retailers (a large clothing retailer and a moderate-size supermaket chain)

Communications Organizations (a large newspaper and a large communications company)

Public Agencies (a large city department, a small state department, and a small federal agency)

Nonprofit Institutions (a small college, a large college, a small arts organization, and a communications organization)
Health Organization (a large hospital)
Public Utility (a large electric company)

This work was financially supported by the Division of Research at the Harvard Business School. I am also in debt to a number of people who contributed helpful ideas along the way, including Renato Tagiuri, Phelps Tracy, the editors of the *Harvard Business Review*, Leonard Schlesinger, Max Hall, Earl Sasser, Chuck Gibson, Joe Seher, William Dowling, Victor Faux, Frank Morgan, Ed Bagley, Michael McCaskey, James Ware, Michael Beer, Jack Gabarro, and Eric Valentine.

Contents

POWER
in
MANAGEMENT

Three important terms defined

The word "power" is used with many different meanings in everyday speech. It would be convenient if one of these meanings were "correct" and the others were wrong. But such is not the case. The more complete dictionaries list all the common meanings, plus some. To minimize confusion, here is the way power will be used in this book:

- *Power* is a measure of a person's potential to get others to do what he or she wants them to do, as well as to avoid being forced by others to do what he or she does not want to do.
- *Power-oriented behavior* refers to individual actions aimed primarily at acquiring or using power.
- *Power dynamics* refers to interpersonal interactions that involve power-oriented behavior.

1

"Power" is an ugly word. It connotes dominance and submission, control and acquiescence, one man's will at the expense of another man's self-esteem. . . . Yet it is power, the ability to control and influence others, that provides the basis for the direction of organizations and for the attainment of social goals. Leadership is the exercise of power.[1]
Abraham Zaleznik and Manfred R. F. Kets de Vries

Power: The neglected aspect of management

Managers regularly acquire and use power. They do so deliberately and consciously as well as intuitively and unconsciously. They utilize a variety of different methods in this pursuit, some of which are well known and some of which are not. Power-oriented behavior can have an impact on managerial career progress, on job performance, on organizational effectiveness, and on the lives of many people. This impact can be small or large; it can be in a direction most people would judge to be good, or in a direction most would say is bad.

In light of these basic facts, it is surprising how little has been written on power and management. In one random sample of ten popular textbooks on management and organizational behavior, I found that less than 3 percent of the material dealt explicitly with the combined topics of power, influence, authority, and organizational politics. Some of those books did not even mention power. Of the roughly two thousand articles

[1]*Power and the Corporate Mind* (Boston: Houghton Mifflin, 1975), p. 3.

1

that appeared in the *Harvard Business Review* between 1955 and 1975, only five, or about one quarter of one percent, had the word "power" in their titles. And, incredibly, the single most influential managerial book to be published recently pays even less attention to power. Peter Drucker's *Management* has over 800 pages, including a 20-page index which references thousands of topics and names. Power does not appear once in that index.

The same vacuum has also historically existed in management education. There are university or industry courses on literally hundreds of managerial topics, but I can remember only once hearing about a course on power and influence.

It is because of this curious inconsistency between the relevance of power to management and the lack of serious discussion of the subject that I have written this book. My purpose is to help managers and students of management to gain a basic understanding of the acquisition and use of power in managerial jobs. I will do so by focusing on questions like these:

—Exactly how do effective managers acquire power?
—How do they use their power?
—For what purposes do they use their power?
—How important to success in management are skills at acquiring and using power?
—What effect does power-oriented behavior have on organizational effectiveness?
—What leads to the misuse of power by managers?
—Specifically how can an appreciation of power dynamics help managers to be more effective?

Of course, with our existing knowledge of power and management, no one can give comprehensive or precise answers to these questions. But one can provide—and I will—basic information which is not intuitively obvious to most managers and which can be very helpful in the performance of managerial jobs.

Ambivalent Attitudes

There are probably many reasons why so little explicit attention has been given to the subject of power dynamics within management. Certainly one major reason is the mixed feelings that Americans, including managers, have about power. On the one hand, most people recognize that power can serve a useful function. They sense, as psychologist Rollo May and others have pointed out, that healthy people almost always have some power that gives them a degree of control over their lives.[2] To be powerless is to be vulnerable to persecution and despair. Most people see that leaders in the economic and political spheres need some power in order to lead, and they feel that leadership is obviously necessary and good. At the extreme, some individuals are absolutely fascinated by power. They sense that power is somehow the key element in the complex puzzle of life, and they are magnetically drawn to it.

But most people have negative feelings about power too. David C. McClelland, the Harvard psychologist, has observed that "in American society in general, individuals are proud of having a high need to Achieve, but dislike being told they have a high need for Power."[3] People often associate power with exploitation and corruption. They tend to distrust people who openly seek power. In some people, this negative attitude toward power is extremely strong. In his enormously popular *The Greening of America*, Charles Reich reflects the views of many when he argues that "it is not the misuse of power that is evil; the very existence of power is evil."[4]

It is not very difficult to see at least some of the origins of these negative attitudes. The United States was born out of a rebellion against power. Since then our public servants seem intent on periodically demonstrating that power can be disas-

[2]*Power and Innocence* (New York: Norton, 1972).
[3]*Power: The Inner Experience* (New York: John Wiley and Sons, 1975), p. 255.
[4]*The Greening of America* (New York: Random House, 1970).

trously misused. At a more personal level, all people have probably at one time in their lives been deeply hurt by a parent, boss, or lover exercising power over them. Such hurt runs deep in many of us, breeding fear and anger. For most people, the net result of both negative and positive attitudes toward power is an awkward ambivalence. Power fascinates and repulses them at the same time.

The ambivalence toward power on the part of managers can be seen in a survey recently reported by Lyman Porter, dean of the School of Management at the University of California, Irvine. One of his students asked a group of managers in an informal questionnaire to describe "organizational politics." Their replies included such positive terms as "important," "challenging," "honest," and "successful," and such negative terms as "repugnant," "threatening," "unfair," and "disliked."[5]

I have seen symptoms of this ambivalence rather often in my work with managers. In seminars, for example, executives seldom discuss how they acquire and use power. Quite the opposite—they often band together to stop such a public discussion. In one session when a manager started to talk about power, the middle-aged top executives present reacted as if he were talking about his sex life. Many participants looked mildly embarrassed, and some quickly moved to change the topic and subtly reprimand the "offender." Yet these same managers were later willing to talk about some aspects of power in a discussion of leadership and motivation (both of which are "good" words that people rarely feel ambivalent about). Furthermore, some of these same managers were also willing to admit to me privately that power dynamics was an important part of their work. A few were even willing to talk about those processes, albeit a bit awkwardly.

[5]"Organizations as Political Animals," presidential address for the Division of Industrial-Organizational Psychology, 84th Annual Meeting of the American Psychological Association, September 4, 1976.

Uncomfortable feelings about power can be seen even more clearly, at least in restrospect, in the management education community. For years, most of those charged with teaching the interpersonal aspects of management—human relations specialists and the like—either adamantly refused to acknowledge the relevance or existence of power or taught others that only "bad" managers tried to acquire and use power. In doing so, they helped reinforce the ambivalance toward power in a generation or two of educated managers.

Ambivalent attitudes toward power, together with the lack of useful information about power and management, breed both naive and cynical beliefs about what effective and successful managers do. These beliefs can be very costly in both career problems and organizational problems.

Many young and well-educated managers, for example, have trouble adjusting to the interpersonal aspects of their new roles. They often do well at analyzing data, thinking through complex possibilities, and identifying alternative actions. But when called upon to choose the best alternative, or to implement it, they do only a fair job at best. In choosing a solution, they often underestimate the difficulty of implementing it (which always involves influencing others). In actually implementing some decision, they tend to be marginally effective in supervising and coordinating others, as well as in keeping their bosses informed (once again, all having to do with influencing people). In both cases, these difficulties can usually be traced to a lack of understanding of power and management and to underdeveloped skills at acquiring power and influencing others.

Of course, some managers receive good advice about power from a boss or a mentor. Or through trial and error they develop an ability to use their personal resources in acquiring and using power. But many other managers receive bad advice from someone who does not understand power dynamics. Or they draw inaccurate conclusions from their own experiences. Either situation can seriously hamper their effectiveness and their career progress.

Even people who are successful early in their careers sometimes fail to continue to grow into positions of greater managerial responsibility because of a lack of appreciation for, or skill at, power-oriented behavior. I have seen many extremely able people lose a key promotion or lose favor with their superiors, marking a turning point in their careers, because of their unrealistic ideas about power. Later I will describe some of these cases in detail. Some young managers are able to learn from—and rebound from—these defeats. Many are not. Some cope with their loss by trading naive for cynical attitudes that further hinder their effectiveness. And they often inadvertently pass those attitudes on to younger managers, thus injuring them too.

In my estimation, most of the managers I have known would be both more effective and more successful if they had a better understanding of power dynamics. For a large number of those managers, perhaps one quarter, the increases in effectiveness and success could be very significant.

Of course, I am not arguing that power skills are all that is necessary for success in management, nor that power is always used for "good" purposes by managers. Because my focus here is on power-oriented behavior, it can sound at times as if I am suggesting that such factors as intelligence, maturity, and hard work are not important in management. They obviously are—but my purpose in this book is not to explore these other factors in depth. My focus here is *only* on power.

Also, because I have chosen to delay a discussion of the misuse of power until Chapter 6, one might think I am suggesting that the methods I describe cannot be misused. They obviously can, and are. But I have chosen not to dwell on this aspect of power early in the book because I think, as David

McClelland has put it, that "America's concern about the possible misuse of power verges at times on a neurotic obsession."[6] I do not want to feed that obsession. Instead, I wish to inform managers and students of management about the need for skillfully executed power-oriented behavior, the positive function such behavior serves, and how it can help organizations, their managers, and society at large.

[6]"The Two Faces of Power," *Journal of International Affairs*, Vol. 24, No. 1 (1970), p. 44.

2

> *The position of a top executive who has little or no equity in the business is often a perilous one, with little inherent security. If things go well, his tenure is usually ensured; if they go badly, all too often he is made the scapegoat. Since many factors that affect his performance are beyond his control, he is constantly subject to the threat of disaster.* [1]
>
> Robert N. McMurry

Power dynamics in management: The basis for its emergence and importance

A number of different rationales have been proposed to explain why power dynamics tend to emerge systematically in managerial processes, what function they serve, and why they are important. Management books that deal with power usually imply that it is an important topic because "formal authority," a type of power, is associated with managerial jobs. Psychologists who have studied managers have said that power is relevant and important because managers tend to have a high "power motivation." Social psychologists and sociologists have noted that power is a relevant managerial topic because power is always an important variable in complex social systems. Contemporary organizations are clearly complex social systems.

[1]"Power and the Ambitious Executive," *Harvard Business Review*, November–December 1973, p. 145.

9

Managers themselves often feel that power is important because "people who don't understand it usually don't get ahead."

In one sense, all these reasons why power is important to managers are correct. But at the same time, the reasons given are misleading in that none of them goes to the real heart of the matter. None of them points directly to the single key reason why power dynamics is an essential aspect of managerial effectiveness. None of them focuses on the *dependence* inherent in managerial jobs.

Dependence in Managerial Jobs

Research by Rosemary Stewart, Leonard Sayles, and others clearly shows that one of the distinguishing characteristics of managerial work, in comparison with other professions, is ceaseless dependence on the activities of a variety of other people.[2] No one stands utterly alone, but the effectiveness of doctors and mathematicians, for example, follows more directly from their own talents and efforts. A manager is more at the mercy of superiors, subordinates, peers in other parts of the organization, subordinates of peers, outside suppliers, customers, competitors, unions, regulating agencies—the list could go on and on.

Although most people recognize that managers "get things done through others," few really appreciate just how much dependence is inherent in managerial jobs. As a successful executive in a large corporation once said to me, "My son, my wife, and many of my professional friends have very inaccurate conceptions of what I really do for a living." He went on to explain:

[2]See Leonard R. Sayles, *Managerial Behavior: Administration in Complex Organization* (New York: McGraw-Hill, 1964); Rosemary Stewart, *Managers and Their Jobs* (London: Macmillan, 1967) and *Contrasts in Management* (London: McGraw-Hill, 1976); and Hugo Uyterhoeven, "General Manager in the Middle," *Harvard Business Review*, March–April 1972.

"Most of these misperceptions are based on the implicit assumption that I somehow have control over all or most of the resources I need to do my job. They think that, much like a skilled cabinetmaker, I have the proper wood, the proper tools, and the time to do good work. In reality, of course, in addition to my direct subordinates, there are hundreds of people whom I have no direct control over but who can affect the performance of my job. At least two dozen of these people are crucial. They control, in a sense, my wood and my tools, and even determine whether I should be making cabinets or boats.

"Some of these crucial people are relatively obvious—the person I report to, for example. But many of them are not. There are, for instance, a number of obscure people on the corporate staff whom I'm very dependent upon. One of them is supervising a construction project right now that is adjacent to one of my facilities. That project can easily create problems for my facility if it isn't managed well. I'm dependent on a few secretaries besides my own. For example, when my boss is out of town, he leaves his secretary essentially in charge. If she makes any poor judgments concerning what she should inform me about, it can hurt me. All this adds up, and leaves me in a much more vulnerable position than most people realize."

Of course, it is possible for a lot of needless dependence to be created by a poor organization structure or poor management practices. One could argue that the manager quoted above was dependent on his boss's secretary because of poor management practices on the part of his superior. But even in cases where the structure and management practices are perfect, a considerable amount of dependence is still an inherent part of managerial jobs—because of two organizational facts of life: division of labor and limited resources. Because the work in organizations is divided into specialized divisions, departments, and jobs, managers are always made directly or indirectly dependent on many others for information, staff services, and cooperation in general. Because of their organization's limited resources, managers are also dependent on their external environments for support. Without some minimum degree of cooperation from suppliers of goods and services, from competitors, unions, regulatory agencies, and customers, managers cannot achieve their objectives and help their organizations prosper.

The Vulnerability of Dependence

Dealing with the vulnerability of dependence is an important yet difficult part of a manager's job. Though it is theoretically possible that all the people and organizations upon which a manager depends would automatically act exactly as the manager wants and needs, such is almost never the case in reality.

All the people on whom a manager is dependent have limited time, energy, and talent, for which there are competing demands. Some people may be uncooperative because they are too busy elsewhere, and some because they are not really capable of helping. Others may well have goals, values, and beliefs that conflict with the manager's and may, therefore, have no desire whatsoever to help or cooperate. This is obviously true of a competing company and sometimes of a union, but it can also apply to a boss who feels threatened by a manager's career progress or to a peer whose objectives clash with the manager's.

Indeed, managers often find themselves dependent on many people (and things) whom they do not directly control and who are not "cooperating." This is the key to one of the biggest frustrations many managers experience in their jobs, even in the top jobs.

Take the case of one moderately large financial services company, which I will call the XYZ Corporation. After nearly a year of rumors, it was finally announced in May 1974 that the president of XYZ had been elected chairman of the board and that Jim Franklin, the vice president of finance, would replace him as president. Although everyone at XYZ had been aware that a shift would take place soon, it had not been at all clear prior to the announcement who would be the next president. Most people had guessed it would be Phil Cook, the marketing vice president.

Shortly after being elected, Franklin tried to bypass what he saw as a potential conflict. He told Cook that he would understand if Cook preferred to move somewhere else where he too could be a chief executive officer. Franklin said that it would be a big loss to the company but that he would be willing to help Cook in a number of ways if he wanted to look for a presidential opportunity elsewhere. Cook thanked him but said that family and community commitments would prevent him from relocating and that all such opportunities were bound to be in a different city.

When Franklin was nine months into his job as chief executive officer, he found that Phil Cook (still the marketing vice president) seemed to be fighting him in small and subtle ways. There was never anything blatant, but Cook just did not cooperate with Franklin as the other vice presidents did.

Since the situation did not improve in the tenth and eleventh months, Franklin seriously considered forcing Cook out. When he thought about the consequences of such a move, however, Franklin became more and more aware of just how dependent he was on Cook. Marketing and sales were generally the keys to success in their industry, and the company's sales force was one of the best, if not the best, in the industry. Cook had been with the company 25 years. He had built a strong personal relationship with many of the people in the sales force and was universally popular. A mass exodus just might occur if Cook were fired. The loss of a large number of salesmen, or even a lot of turmoil in the department, could have a serious effect on the company's performance. Under those circumstances, the board of directors might ask Franklin to resign or step aside.

When I last spoke with Franklin he had been chief executive officer for one year. At that time he said that the situation between Cook and himself had not improved and had become a constant source of frustration. "I am not accomplishing as much as I should," he told me, "and that is primarily because of Cook."

As a person gains more formal authority in an organization, the areas in which he or she is vulnerable increase and become more complex rather than the reverse. As the previous example suggests, it is not at all unusual for the president of an organization to be in a highly dependent position, a fact often not apparent to those who covet the president's job. And that dependence can and does occasionally lead to firings, demotions, and other unpleasant situations which, from the point of view of the managers involved, can look very unfair. As one top executive put it, "At times I feel like nothing more than an easy target for every disgruntled or ambitious or incompetent person I know." A recent survey of nearly 400 chief executive officers suggests that this feeling may be widely shared. One in three of them reported that he thinks about sudden or unexpected removal from office several times a year.[3]

Coping with Dependence

Some excellent work by Professor Henry Mintzberg has shown rather clearly that effective managers often behave in ways that are different from what traditional management texts suggest.[4]

[3] Survey conducted by John Arnold ExecuTrak Systems (reported in the *Boston Globe*, August 19, 1977).
[4] See Henry Mintzberg, "The Manager's Job: Folklore and Fact," *Harvard Business Review*, July–August 1975, p. 49.

I think that much of this inexplicable behavior becomes understandable in light of a manager's need to manage his or her dependence on others. To be able to plan, organize, budget, staff, control, and evaluate, managers need some control over the many people on whom they are dependent. Yet managerial jobs *do not* automatically provide managers with that control.

Trying to control others solely on the basis of the power associated with one's position simply will not work—first, because managers are always dependent on some people over whom they have no formal authority and, second, because almost no one in modern organizations will passively accept and completely obey a constant stream of orders from someone just because he or she is the "boss."

Some people would argue that managers can get control of their jobs if only they would communicate more. But a careful examination of managerial work shows that good communication, while clearly helpful, has its limitations. It requires time, for example, often lots of it. The other people must be willing to listen. And the others actually must agree to act on the new information in the way the manager desires.

This is not to say that directing people through the formal power of one's position and good communication are not important means by which successful managers cope. They obviously are. But, even taken together, they are not usually enough. One high-level financial executive made the point this way:

"Employee willingness to defer to you just because you are 'the boss' has gone down steadily in the past two decades. This is especially true of young people, who do not automatically respect authority the way their parents did. At the same time, the number of people who can affect a manager's performance, but yet do not directly report to him, has also gone up. For example, we didn't have a computer department 15 years ago;

but today we do, and it does work for me that my own people used to do.

"Up to a point you can cope with the situation today by communicating more with people, by convincing them that it makes sense to do what you need them to do. This is crucial, but it works only up to a point. When I go over and tell the head of the computer group 14 reasons why he should speed up the reports coming to us, he sometimes gives me 15 reasons why that is not possible. So I come out of that meeting with nothing gained, and with one half-hour less time to do my job. To deal with this situation, you have got to find other ways to get people to cooperate."

The Necessary Emergence of Power Dynamics

What are those other ways? Considerable evidence, accumulated by observing and talking with such managers, suggests that successful managers cope with their dependence on others by being sensitive to it, by eliminating or avoiding *unnecessary* dependence, and by establishing countervailing power over those others. Good managers then use that power to help them plan, organize, staff, budget, motivate, and evaluate. Figure 1 lays out the situation.

Without the skillful acquisition and use of power, managers are seldom able to cope effectively with their dependence on others; the dependence in their jobs is just too great, and their automatic control over it is far too little. They need additional power and ability to use it so as to influence others to cooperate. *In other words, the primary reason power dynamics emerge and play an important role in organizations is not necessarily because managers are power hungry, or because they want desperately to get ahead, or because there is an inherent conflict between managers who have authority and workers who do not. It is because the dependence inherent in managerial jobs is greater than the power or control given to the people in those jobs.*

Power dynamics, under these circumstances, are inevitable and are needed to make organizations function well.

The rather extreme example of Jerry Donatur and Dave Hirsch shows why power dynamics inevitably emerge and why they are important to effective management. Jerry and Dave were business school classmates. They were equally bright, personable, and energetic. Their first jobs after graduation were similar, and they both had a basic understanding of modern managerial tools and analytical techniques. Yet, after one year on the job, they found themselves in very different situations.

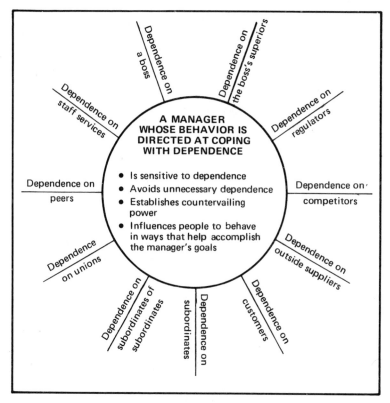

Figure 1. Coping with job-related dependence.

A visitor to Dave's department would have seen a situation right out of the pages of a textbook on good management. The department had a clear set of short- and long-range plans. It was logically organized and staffed with a group of obviously talented and motivated people. A number of different information and control systems helped Dave and others to monitor the department's effectiveness, which was high on all measures. Dave enjoyed the respect of both his supervisor and his subordinates, who felt he was largely responsible for the department's effectiveness.

A visit to Jerry's department would have found almost the opposite situation. Virtually no planning was being done. The organization was chaotic, morale was low, and turnover was high. The few information and control systems that existed were largely ignored, except by Jerry. The department was over budget and was performing poorly on almost all standards. Jerry's superiors were upset and were about to fire him.

A look at the events that led up to these situations can help us understand the very different results. Both Dave and Jerry began to work at about the same time. Their jobs were comparable in many ways; for example, both jobs made them dependent on a similar set of people. But their approaches to their jobs varied considerably.

Before starting his job, Dave spent time doing some homework on his new department. In this effort he learned many things, including the chief complaint voiced by those working in the department ("not enough office space") and the most visible weakness in the department's performance ("poor planning results in people becoming overwhelmed with work three or four times a year"). He also took some time to develop his relationship with the company president, who had interviewed him during the recruiting process. In his final discussion with the president before starting work, he brought up what he thought were the legitimate complaints about office space and received a commitment to increase the department's office space by about 30 percent.

Because Dave had made an impression on the president even before starting work, in his first week on the job the president stopped by to see him for a few minutes. His new subordinates were in awe: no one could remember the president ever coming into the department before. Dave also made the announcement about the office space. His employees were elated.

In his first two months on the job, Dave concentrated on developing good relations with his subordinates, his boss, and others he needed to depend upon. He also devoted his attention to finding an easy way to make some progress on the planning/scheduling problem faced by the department. And he eventually did find a way. By applying some simple tools learned in graduate school, he was able to schedule work assignments so as to significantly reduce the next peak work period. Implementing the new schedule was easy, because he avoided changes that could have upset people.

During his tenth week, the annual "end of August chaos" didn't happen. There was still an increase in work, and a decrease in the department's ability to respond quickly, but the normal peak with its associated problems disappeared. The improvement was very visible—to the department's employees, to other departments, and to upper management. All were impressed.

In less than four months on the job Dave established such a strong power position that he was able to convince his boss that he needed two extra staff positions, above and beyond the budget. And he was able to get most of his subordinates to work harder and more systematically.

Dave's fifth through twelfth months on the job progressed in a similar way. He continued to build good relationships with those around him. He continued to receive more resources to help him do his job. Each month he took on more difficult problems, but only after he felt he had the power to solve them. In the fifth and sixth months he developed and implemented new information and control systems. In the seventh and eighth months he reorganized the department. In the ninth month he fired one person and transferred another out of his department.

At the end of the first year, Dave had a department that was a model for others. And he was able to maintain that well-managed operation because, as one of his peers noted, "he's in a very powerful position."

Jerry began work without doing any of the homework Dave did. The first month on the job he spent most of his time learning his department's activities and identifying its problems. In this, he was able to successfully apply his education and his intelligence. Within 60 days Jerry had a thorough understanding of his group's strengths and weaknesses.

After 90 days, Jerry announced a basic reorganization of the department, fired one of his employees, and requested permission from his boss to add one new lower-level position. He immediately received word that his boss wanted to talk to him about these plans. The subsequent discussion was a difficult one; his boss expressed concern over his plans and asked a long list of tough questions, some of which Jerry was unprepared for. As a result of the meeting, Jerry was asked to delay making any changes until his boss could study his plans more carefully.

Jerry had to announce to his employees that the changes would not be implemented immediately. His relations with his people, which had been cordial up to that point, began to deteriorate rapidly. New problems began to emerge in his department. Jerry pointed to these problems as evidence that his changes were very much needed. But his boss was unimpressed.

In his sixth month Jerry received a scathing memo from another department manager (with a copy to his and Jerry's boss) complaining about some of the work Jerry's department had recently completed. This created a minor crisis; the series of meetings that followed absorbed much of Jerry's time for the next month.

In his eighth month two of his department's employees sent an anonymous complaint to Jerry's boss regarding the management of the department. This letter set in motion another series of meetings that absorbed much of Jerry's time for the next two months.

By the twelfth month the situation had degenerated even further. Jerry fully realized he was in a hopeless position ("I have trouble even getting a letter typed around here") and was looking for a job on the outside.

This disappointing first step in Jerry's career might have been avoided if he had approached his job as Dave did. By systematically developing power and then using it to influence those he needed to depend upon, Dave was able to manage his department effectively. Jerry's lack of power essentially made it impossible for him to manage his department.

In similar ways, some power is always necessary for effective management. Without sufficient power, a manager is at the mercy of those he or she is dependent upon and will never be able to effectively plan, organize, control, motivate, and evaluate. As such, it is hardly surprising that power dynamics emerge as an important aspect of managerial work.

Power Needs and the Degree of a Manager's Dependence

An argument that took place during a middle-management training seminar a few years ago helps illustrate the important relationship between managers' need for power and the degree of their dependence on others.

Two participants, both managers in their thirties, got into a heated disagreement regarding the acquisition and use of power by managers. One said that power was virtually irrelevant; the other argued that it was absolutely central to managerial work. Each combatant, in support of his position, described a "very successful" manager with whom he worked: One manager seemed to be continually developing and using power, whereas the other rarely did so. Later, both seminar participants were asked to describe their successful managers' jobs in terms of the dependence inherent in those jobs.

The participant who felt power was unimportant described a staff vice president in a small company who was dependent only on his immediate subordinates, his peers, and his boss. This person, Joe Phillips, had to depend on his subordinates to do their jobs appropriately. But if necessary he could fill in for any of them or replace them rather easily. He also had extensive formal authority over them; he could give them raises and new assignments, recommend promotions, and fire them. He was moderately dependent on the other four vice presidents in the company for information and cooperation. They were likewise dependent on him. The president had considerable formal authority over Phillips but was also dependent on him for help, expert advice, the services of his staff, information, and general cooperation.

The second participant—the one who felt that power was very important—described a service department manager, Sam Weller, who was in a significantly different position in a large, complex, and growing company. Weller was dependent not only on his boss, for rewards and information, but also on 30 other individuals who made up the divisional and corporate top management. And though his boss, like Phillips', was moderately dependent on him too, most of the top managers were not. Because Weller's subordinates, unlike Phillips', had people reporting to them, Weller was dependent not only on his subordinates but also on his subordinates' subordinates. Because he himself could not easily replace them or do most of their technical jobs, he was very dependent on all these people.

In addition, for critical supplies Weller was dependent on two other department managers in the division. Without their timely help, it was impossible for his department to do its job. These departments, however, did not have similar needs for Weller's help and cooperation. Weller was also dependent on local labor union officials and on a federal agency that regulated the division's industry. Both could shut his division down if they wanted. Finally, Weller was dependent on two outside suppliers of key materials. Because the volume of his department's purchases was small relative to the size of these two companies, he had little power over them.

Under these circumstances, Sam Weller had to spend much time acquiring and using power while Joe Phillips did not. Weller's job put him in a position where he was much more dependent on others and needed much more power-oriented behavior to manage that dependence.

Of course, if most management jobs were like Phillips', instead of Weller's, the question of power would not be that important. But most management jobs are more like Weller's than Phillips'. Although some people might argue that organizations should be redesigned so that management jobs are more like Phillips', the trend over the past two or three decades is clearly in the opposite direction.

Technological advances, the growth of organizations, raw materials cartels, and greater government activity all tend to increase the dependence inherent in managerial jobs. Sources of external dependence, in particular, have multiplied in the past decade. At the same time, the increasingly negative attitude toward authority figures on the part of employees is reducing the power that automatically goes with a managerial job. Since all these trends are likely to continue, it will be more and more difficult to design management jobs in which the authority is equal to the responsibility. Under these conditions, power dynamics will necessarily be even more important in complex organizations. And the effective acquisition and use of power by managers will become even more essential.

3

Basic methods for acquiring and maintaining power

Most people who have achieved some success in managerial jobs use similar methods, in varying degrees, for acquiring power. Some of these methods seem to be simply "good management practice." Other methods, as we shall see in this chapter, appear to be what textbooks would often describe as "bad management." Still other methods might seem to many people, at least at first glance, rather unethical. Let us try to set aside for the moment any idea of how managers *ought* to behave and examine only how they *do* behave in their quest for power. Later we can explore the consequences of these behaviors.

Gaining Control over Tangible Resources

Acquiring power means acquiring *potential* influence—that is, the potential for getting others to do what you want or for

[1] In an interview with the author.

preventing them from forcing you to do something. Perhaps the most obvious way in which managers develop such potential is by gaining direct control over tangible resources—such as budgets, employees, buildings, and equipment.

The often told story of wartime supply sergeants, whose control of large quantities of scarce goods made them more powerful than most colonels, is based on fact. Resources clearly put a manager in a better position to influence others and to acquire other types of power.

Much of the time managers gain control over resources simply by performing their jobs in ways their superiors judge to be particularly good. Resources tend to flow to high achievers. We saw a clear case of this with Dave Hirsch in the previous chapter. His good performance allowed him to receive additional staff positions.

Managers gain control of resources in other ways too. A commonly used tactic is to identify and acquire a managerial position that may not formally seem very powerful but that can potentially control many scarce resources (such as the supply sergeant's position). As one manager in a health care organization explained:

"In 1969 I took a low-level managerial job at the Redding Hospital. In 1970 I requested and obtained a transfer to a similar job in a different part of the hospital. The good track record I established my first year allowed me to ask for and be seriously considered for the transfer. But I received the transfer mainly because no one comparable wanted the job. My request for the transfer was based on my analysis of a number of important changes that were occurring back then. I recognized that changes within the medical profession and in federal laws were going to make a considerable amount of money available to one obscure department in the hospital. So when the manager of that department was promoted, I requested that job.

"My analysis proved to be correct. As a result, I have been able to increase that department's budget over the past three years by over 2,000 percent. And in the process, I have become one of the most powerful people in the hospital."

Similarly, powerful managers gain control of resources by being sensitive to the effect on resources of *all* the decisions they make. They do not inadvertently give away the store.

Obtaining Information and Control of Information Channels

A second way in which managers can acquire power is through the control of useful information and information channels. In a complex society or organization, information can be even more important than traditional tangible resources, because rational problem solving and influence by persuasion are essential in complex settings. The control of scarce information—on what motivates specific people, for instance, or on outcomes or processes related to organizational goals—can enhance one's problem-solving ability. Thus information is power.

One manager who has acquired considerable power through gaining control of information and information channels is Barry Edwards. In 1971, Barry accepted an offer to leave his employer of ten years and become the vice president of finance for a moderate-size manufacturing firm in a relatively mature industry. As is often the case with new executives, his real power in the company was relatively low at first, despite his formal position. But this situation changed dramatically within a nine-month period. In his eighth month on the job insiders agreed that Edwards had become as powerful as the company president.

Edwards gained his power primarily in two ways. First, he and his staff developed six new information-control systems whose output went to him. These systems reported costs for each product line, spoilage for each plant, and quality of manpower in each major department. Second, he spent a considerable amount of time getting acquainted with people in all parts of the company, and then calling on them regularly to learn what was happening in their area. Because he had control of these formal and informal information systems Edwards almost always had better data than anyone else on most major corporate activities. With this information he became the most influential individual in corporate affairs.

Of course, not all kinds of information provide an equal amount of power. Some types of information, because of their scarcity and their relevance, are much more important than others. (The same can be said for tangible resources.) People who are particularly successful at gaining power by the control of information tend to have certain competences which help them to identify relevant data.

For instance, Barry Edwards was a very competent business and financial analyst. His analytical skills helped him to design the formal information systems and to ask others relevant questions informally. But his awareness of power dynamics motivated him to create and use those systems—no one, not even his boss, had asked him to do so. Edwards' case is a good example of how technical competence, in combination with power awareness and skills, can lead to success.

Establishing Favorable Relationships

Another set of methods which managers use to acquire power focuses on relationships. These methods are probably less well understood than those involving resource control, but they may be more important overall.

Acquiring power through relationships is basically an exercise in developing some type of *credibility*. This credibility can be established in a number of different ways, but it always involves another's willingness to defer to the manager within certain bounds. Such relationships help managers to influence those they must depend upon. They also provide managers with indirect access to other people's tangible resources and information.

Creating a sense of obligation

One way in which a manager can establish favorable relationships with other people is by getting them to feel obligated in certain ways.

For example, managers will sometimes do favors for people who they expect will feel obliged to return them. Some people are very skilled at identifying opportunities for doing favors that may not be very costly but are nevertheless greatly appreciated. One such manager, according to a subordinate, is so good at this tactic that "most of the people here would walk over hot coals in their bare feet if my boss asked them to."

How does he do it? "He really knows how to use his charm to make them feel good. And he has an incredible capacity to do little things that mean a lot to people. Today, for example, in his junk mail he came across an advertisement for something that one of my subordinates had in passing once mentioned that he was shopping for. So my boss routed it to him. That probably took 15 seconds of his time, but my subordinate really appreciated it. To give you another example, two weeks ago he somehow learned that the purchasing manager's mother had died. On his way home that night, he stopped off at the funeral parlor. Our purchasing manager was, of course, there at the time. I bet he'll remember that brief visit for a while."

Recognizing that most people believe friendship carries with it certain obligations, managers sometimes try to develop friendships, especially with powerful superiors. They will also make formal and informal deals in which they make concessions in exchange for certain future obligations. And they often look for ways to make their employees feel obliged to defer to their formal authority. For example, a manager might sit down with employees who are new or with people who are starting new projects and reach an agreement with them regarding who has the formal authority to do what—thus creating a strong sense of obligation in them to defer to the manager's authority later.

Of course, powerful managers seldom if ever make friendships, form alliances, or do favors for others *just* to gain power. Like all people, they usually engage in a specific act for numerous reasons. The manager who visited the funeral parlor could easily have done so for altruistic, organizational, *and* self-centered reasons. One of the characteristics of many successful managers is that they can identify and implement actions that are good for both them and their organizations.

Building a good professional reputation

Another way to gain power through relationships is by building a reputation as an expert in certain matters. People will often defer to the manager because they believe in the manager's expertise.

This type of power is usually established through visible achievement. The larger and more visible the achievement, the more power the individual tends to develop. Visibility is especially important in large settings, where most people have only secondhand information about the professional competence of others.

The importance of visibility is particularly clear in the case of Herb Randley and Bert Kline, both 35-year-old vice presidents in a large research and development organization. According to their closest associates, they were equally bright and competent in their technical fields and as managers. Yet Randley had a much stronger professional reputation in most parts of the company, and his ideas generally carried much more weight. Close friends and associates claim that Randley's superior power was related to a number of tactics he used to develop highly visible achievements.

Randley had published more scientific papers and managerial articles than Kline. Randley had been more selective in the assignments he had worked on, choosing those that were visible and that required his strong suits. He had given more speeches and presentations on projects that were his own achievements. In meetings, he was forceful in areas where he had expertise and silent in those where he did not.

The power that comes from valuable—and visible—achievements is crucial for success in most managerial jobs. In most organizations this type of power is probably more important today than it was 30 or 40 years ago. Today's better-educated managerial workforce has a greater respect for expertise. And today's technologically complex organization obviously has greater need for it.

Encouraging identification

Managers also gain power in relationships by fostering others' unconscious identification with them or with ideas they "stand for." This form of power is most clearly seen in the way people relate to charismatic leaders. Generally, the more a person idealizes a manager, both consciously and (more important) unconsciously, the more he or she will defer to that manager.

Managers develop power based on others' idealized views of them in a number of ways. They try to look and behave in ways that others respect. They go out of their way to be visible to their employees and to give speeches about organizational goals, values, and ideals. They even consider, while making hiring and promotion decisions, whether they will be able to develop this type of power over the candidates.

One vice president of sales in a moderate-size service company had worked his way up "from nothing" after immigrating to the United States at age 17. When he became a sales manager in 1965, he began recruiting other young immigrants and sons of immigrants from his former country. He continued to do so after he became vice president of sales in 1970. In 1975, about 85 percent of his sales force was made up of people whom he hired directly or who were hired by others he brought in. His power over these employees, based primarily on their strong identification with him and what he stood for, was very strong. In his industry he was reputed to be so much in control of his sales force that he could get them to respond to new and different marketing programs in a third of the time taken by the company's best competitors.

Although this method of developing power is probably more important to elected officials than managers, it plays a key role in most organizations. People generally need to look up to someone who can make them feel strong and confident despite all the problems that they face, and who can help them feel they are doing something meaningful—especially if their jobs seem trivial or pointless. Managers who can fill these needs can become very powerful.

Creating perceived dependence

Managers often gain power in relationships by feeding others' beliefs that they are dependent on the managers for either help or security. The more dependent other people perceive themselves to be, the more they will be inclined to cooperate with such managers.

Managers often use two methods to create perceived dependence. In the first, the manager controls resources which others need but which they neither possess nor can readily acquire elsewhere. Then the manager makes sure they perceive that he or she can use such resources to help or hinder them.

Consider the following extreme—but true—example. When Tim Babcock was put in charge of a division of a large manufacturing company and told to "turn it around," he spent the first few weeks studying the situation. He decided that the division was in disastrous shape and that he needed to take major steps quickly to save it. He realized he had to develop considerable power fast over most of the division's management and staff. So he did the following:

—He gave the division's management two hours' notice of his arrival.

—He arrived in a limousine with six assistants.

—He immediately called a meeting of the top 40 managers.

—He outlined briefly his assessment of the situation, his commitment to turn things around, and the basic direction he wanted things to move in.

—He then fired the four top managers in the room and told them to be out of the building in two hours.

—He then said he would personally dedicate himself to sabotaging the career of anyone who tried to block his efforts to save the division.

—He ended the 60-minute meeting by announcing that his assistants would set up appointments for him with each of them starting at 7:00 A.M. the next morning.

Throughout the critical six-month period that followed, those who remained at the division generally cooperated energetically with Mr. Babcock.

A second way in which managers gain this type of power is by influencing other people's perceptions of a manager's resources. In settings where many people are involved and where the manager does not interact continually with those he or she is dependent on, people will seldom possess hard facts regarding what relevant resources the manager commands directly or indirectly through others, what resources the manager might command in the future, or how prepared he or she is to use those resources to help or hinder them. They will be forced to make their own judgments. Managers, insofar as they can influence people's judgments, can generate much more power than one would generally ascribe to them on the basis of the reality of their resources.

In trying to influence people's judgment, some managers pay considerable attention to the trappings of power. They sometimes carefully select, decorate, and arrange their offices in ways that give signs of power. They associate with people or organizations that are known or supposed to be powerful. They even selectively foster rumors about their power.

Bill Jennings gained power in this way. Despite the fact that he was the manager of only a relatively minor division in a large and diversified corporation, he was alleged to be even more powerful than many of his bosses. The reason? "He seems to have a strong and unique relationship with the chairman of the board," one of his peers told me. "They have lunch together rather often, and he seems to work on special assignments for the chairman. Most of us think he has already been selected to run the company someday. Whether we are right or not nobody knows, but no one I know is about to risk upsetting Jennings, and a lot of people go out of their way to cooperate with him in any way they can."

Keys to Success at Acquiring Power

Managers who are particularly successful at acquiring and maintaining power do not necessarily use all the methods described in this chapter to the same degree or in the same way. Nevertheless, such managers do share a number of important characteristics.

1. *They tend to be very sensitive to where power exists in their organizations.*

Successful managers go far beyond formal organization charts and job descriptions to learn who really controls resources and information, what the important interpersonal relationships are, and what people they are really dependent upon. They are politically sensitive, because they have to be. Without this information, they cannot acquire power efficiently. Too much time and effort would be wasted looking for resources in the wrong places and developing relationships with the wrong people. In addition, they might accidentally offend a very powerful person or a key individual who must be depended upon.

2. *To some degree, they use all the methods described in this chapter to develop power.*

Of course, some may use certain methods much more frequently than others. But unlike managers who are less successful at developing power, they do not assume that some of the methods are ineffective or that some are "immoral." They intuitively recognize that all these methods can, under certain circumstances, provide them with necessary power. Furthermore, they recognize that ignoring any method inevitably means reducing the amount of power that can be developed, reducing their ability to get things done, and putting themselves in a more vulnerable position.

3. *They take calculated risks in which they "invest" some of their power in the hopes of gaining it back with interest.*

Edward Banfield, a political scientist, first reported that successful politicians used power in a way that was similar to how successful entrepreneurs used capital. The politicians took risks, investing their power in decisions and actions in the hopes of getting even more in return.[2] I believe the same is true for most successful managers.

Mark Schechtman is typical in this regard. During a three-year period Mark increased his power considerably by first seeking and obtaining a transfer into an area that he knew was critical to the company's five-year growth plans. He was put in charge of a construction project, where he used all the power he

---

[2]See *Political Influence* (New York: Free Press, 1975), Chapter 11.

had to finish the project one day ahead of schedule. This cost him a significant investment of power but led directly to a large increase in his professional reputation, the development of a strong mentor relationship with a vice president, and a promotion in the same area. He gained more formal authority, more responsibilities, more tangible assets, and the control of some new information channels. He quickly used these additional resources to develop even more power. For example, he used his new mentor relationship to help develop more favorable realtionships with some of his peers who felt more dependent on him because of his "in" with top management. He then used this additional power to exceed his financial and other objectives for the year. This accomplishment led to still another promotion.

Of course, even the most skillful managers will occasionally invest some power and not get any return. Such is the nature of risk taking in any activity.

   4. They recognize that all of their actions can affect their power and they avoid actions that will accidentally decrease it.

Managers who are effective at acquiring power tend to calculate the consequences of any action not only in terms of its organizational impact but also in terms of its effect on their power. (See Figure 2.) Most do so not because they always wish to select the option that maximizes their power, but because they want to know the price they will probably pay to achieve certain organizational objectives. They recognize that power is too valuable to be wasted.

   5. In their career development they try to move both up the hierarchy and toward positions where they can control some strategic contingency for their organization.[3]

Managers who are particularly good at acquiring and main-

---

[3]For a good discussion of this point see G. Salancik and J. Pfeffer, "Who Gets Power—and How They Hold On to It: A Strategic-Contingency Model of Power," *Organizational Dynamics*, Winter 1977.

taining power recognize that to maintain increasing power it must be occasionally consolidated. This means using it to gain a higher formal position. It is virtually impossible to keep acquiring more and more power in a low-level management position or to maintain a significant amount of power in such a position.

Perhaps even more important, powerful managers gain and maintain really sizable amounts of power by moving into positions that control key contingencies for their organizations. If, for example, technical product innovation were the "name of the game" in their industry, they would probably move into research and development management. If selling were most important, they would move up the ranks of sales management. They do so because they recognize that as long as their organization has to compete with others to get support from its environment, those who can manage the most problematic environmental contingencies are really the most important people in the organization. Everyone, in a sense, must depend on those individuals. And that situation gives them a great deal of power.

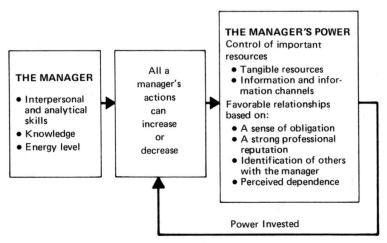

Figure 2. Managerial behavior and the acquisition of power.

4

To be successful in using power you have to have a sense *of power. I would define that as a gut feel of being able to predict with some degree of certainty how people will react in certain situations, so you can predict when there is going to be trouble over something. You also need an understanding of what motivates people in a positive sense, and in a pejorative sense, you need manipulative skills.* [1]

W. Michael Blumenthal, Secretary of the Treasury
(former president and chairman of the Bendix Corporation)

Basic methods for using power to influence others

Effective managers use power to influence others. These people include superiors, subordinates, peers, and outsiders—people whom managers must depend upon because of the very nature of their managerial jobs. In influencing such people, managers use a number of different direct and indirect methods, most of which are well known. (See Figure 3.) Much less understood, however, are exactly how and when these methods are used.

As in the previous chapter, our focus here will be on how influential managers actually *do* behave, not on how we think they *should* behave. Later we will explore the consequences of this behavior.

[1]Quoted in Michael Korda, *Power: How to Get It, How to Use It* (New York: Random House, 1975), p. 38.

Figure 3.

Direct Methods	What They Can Influence
Exercise the power in a relationship, based on • An obligation	Behavior within zone that the other perceives as legitimate in light of the obligation.
• A good professional reputation	Attitudes and behavior within the zone of perceived expertise.
• Identification with a manager	Attitudes and behavior that are not in conflict with the ideals that underlie the identification.
• Perceived dependence	Wide range of behavior that can be monitored.
Coercively exercise relationship power based on perceived dependence.	Very wide range of behavior that can be easily monitored.
Use information to persuade others.	Very wide range of attitudes and behavior.
Use resources to obtain the compliance of others.	Wide range of behavior that can be monitored.
Combine these methods.	Depends on the exact combination.
Indirect Methods	* * *
Manipulate the other's environment by using any or all of the face-to-face methods.	Wide range of behavior and attitudes.
Change the forces that continuously act on the individual: • Formal organizational setups • Informal social arrangements • Technology • Resources available • Statement of organizational goals	Wide range of behavior and attitudes on a continuous basis.

Methods of Influence

Advantages	Drawbacks
Quick. Requires no outlay of tangible resources.	If the request is outside the acceptable zone, it will fail; if it is too far outside, others might see it as illegitimate.
Quick. Requires no outlay of tangible resources.	If the request is outside the acceptable zone, it will fail; if it is too far outside, others might see it as illegitimate.
Quick. Requires no outlay of tangible resources.	Restricted to influence attempts that are not in conflict with the ideals that underlie the identification.
Quick. Can often succeed when other methods fail.	Repeated influence attempts encourage the other to gain power over the influencer.
Quick. Can often succeed when other methods fail.	Invites retaliation. Very risky. Other person may not follow through.
Can produce internalized motivation that does not require monitoring. Requires no power or outlay of scarce material resources.	Can be very time-consuming. Requires other person to listen.
Can succeed when using power in a relationship and persuasion are not feasible or attractive.	Can be expensive. Often seen as illegitimate.
Can be more potent and less risky than using a single method.	More costly than using a single method.
* * *	* * *
Can succeed when face-to-face methods fail.	Can be time-consuming. Complex to implement. Very risky, especially if used frequently.
Has continuous influence, not just a one-shot effect. Can have a very powerful impact.	Often requires a considerable power outlay to achieve.

Direct Influence

Exercising the Power in Relationships

If power exists in a relationship and the manager correctly understands the nature and strength of it, he can influence others directly (face to face or on the phone) with nothing more than a brief request or command. The chief advantage of this approach is speed. The ability to influence someone *quickly* can be enormously important to managers, who are often pressed for time. Thus this method is used often in complex modern organizations. For example:

- Jones knows Smith feels obliged to him for past favors. Furthermore, Jones thinks that his request to speed up a project by two days probably falls within a zone that Smith would consider legitimate in light of his sense of obligation to Jones. So Jones simply calls Smith and makes his request. Smith pauses for only a second and says yes, he'll do it.
- Manager Johnson has some power based on perceived dependence over manager Baker. When Johnson tells Baker that he wants a report done in 24 hours, Baker considers the costs of compliance, of noncompliance, and of complaining to higher authorities. He decides that doing the report is the least costly action and tells Johnson he will do it.
- Young Porter identifies strongly with Marquette, an older manager who is not his boss. Porter thinks Marquette is the epitome of a great manager and tries to model himself after him. When Marquette asks Porter to work on a special project "that could be very valuable in improving the company's ability to meet new competitive products," Porter agrees without hesitation and works 15 hours a week beyond his normal time to get the project done and done well.

When used to influence others, each type of relationship-based power has somewhat different advantages and drawbacks. For example, power based on a professional reputation or on identification with a manager can often be used to influence attitudes as well as someone's immediate behavior and thus can have a lasting impact. Influencing attitudes by using power based on perceived dependence is difficult. But at the same time, power based on perceived dependence usually has the advantage of being able to influence a broader range of behavior than the other methods do. When exercising power based on a professional reputation, for example, one can influence only attitudes and behavior within the narrow zone defined by the perceived expertise. A sensitivity to these and other nuances is important for success in using power.

One unusually sensitive, perceptive, and articulate manager described his use of power in relationships as such:

"I have very strong relationships with most of the people I work with. These relationships are a very important source of power, but they don't guarantee me influence. You have got to have a correct sense of each relationship and each person in order to know how to use the power effectively. . . . My relationship with Phil George is based mostly on his respect for my marketing skills [a good professional reputation]. As such, if I wanted, I could tell Phil that he should clear his calendar for the next three days and rethink the marketing part of his business plan and he'd probably do it. But if I told him to clear his calendar and redo the manufacturing plan, it wouldn't work. As a matter of fact, he would probably be both surprised and upset if I made that request."

But, he went on to point out, his relationships with some other people were very different and allowed him different opportunities for influence. "In Dan Salerno's case, my relationship is based mostly on his clear understanding that I can make life for him around here easy or difficult [perceived dependence]. Now I could tell Dan to go out and wax my car and he'd probably do it. But if I told him to spend a few days and rethink something—some aspect of a marketing program or whatever—he would say yes. But he probably wouldn't do it.

He would just tell me he did, and thank me for the advice."

The drawbacks associated with the use of power based on perceived dependence are particularly important to recognize. A person who feels dependent on a manager for rewards (or lack of punishments) might quickly agree to a request from the manager but then not follow through—especially if the manager cannot easily find out if the person has obeyed or not. Repeated influence attempts based on perceived dependence also seem to encourage the other person to try to gain some power to balance the manager's. And perhaps most important, using power based on perceived dependence in a coercive way is very risky. Coercion invites retaliation.

For instance, in the example from Chapter 3 in which Tim Babcock took such extreme steps to save the division he was assigned to "turn around," his development and coercive use of power based on perceived dependence could have led to mass resignations and the collapse of the division. Babcock recognized that risk, however, and behaved as he did because he felt there was simply no other way that he could gain the very large amount of quick cooperation needed to save the division. And that is not unusual. Time pressures often force managers to rely on some form of coercion.

Persuasion and other methods

In addition to exercising the power in relationships, managers influence others directly by using information to persuade them, by using resources to buy their compliance, and by combining these and other methods.

The key to persuasion usually lies in having and knowing how to use information that is relevant to another person's interests and goals. An influential manager tends to be very skilled at identifying and communicating information to another person that "makes sense" and that leads to changes in the person's beliefs and behavior that the manager desires.

For example, a persuasive manager will use information:

- To convince people that some action (which the manager desires) is in their best interests while other actions are not.
- To motivate people (in a direction the manager wants) by showing them that they can achieve something they wish or that they can contribute to something they believe in.
- To help people by demonstrating how they can achieve some end that they (and the manager) wish to achieve.

Persuasion can be unusually influential because it can affect a wide range of attitudes and behavior and produce internalized motivation that does not require monitoring or follow-up. But persuasion has a number of serious drawbacks that are often not recognized, especially by well-educated people. Persuasion can be very time-consuming. And it can be completely ineffective if people are not willing to listen. "Our R&D manager fails in his efforts to influence others about half the time," one production manager reported, "because he always tries to persuade them—logically. Sometimes I think that if he were attacked by a lion he would try to talk the beast out of injuring him."

Using resources to buy another person's compliance, on the other hand, can succeed when persuasion and other methods fail. "We were told when we bought one Midwestern newspaper," a corporate president reported, "that it would be impossible to convince the local union to allow the changes that were needed to make the paper economically viable. But we did. All it took was a lot of money—a single cash payment for everyone in the local. People thought we were nuts. But the $2 million investment, combined with another $2 million in new equipment, has allowed us to eliminate 75 percent of the production jobs. This has reduced our yearly operating expenses by over $1 million. Our total investment will be paid back in less than four years, and we are going to have a very profitable property."

Nevertheless, buying compliance has its obvious drawbacks.

It can often be too expensive, and it can be seen as illegitimate. "One of the managers in the computer group told me if I would do something for him he would give me ten free hours on the machine," a middle-level executive once reported with a look of disbelief. "I threw him out of my office."

Perhaps most often, managers draw on more than one of the methods described above to influence someone. In general, they do so because a combination can be more potent and less risky than any single method, as the following comment shows: "One of the best managers we have in the company has lots of power based on one thing or another. But he seldom if ever just tells or asks someone to do something. He almost always takes a few minutes to try to persuade them. The relationships he has with people generally induce them to listen carefully and certainly dispose them to be influenced. That, of course, makes the persuasion process go quickly and easily. And he never risks getting the other person mad or upset by making what that person thinks is an unfair request or command."

This combined use of relationship-based power and persuasion is enormously important in most organizations today. The complex and competitive environments in which organizations live require that the contribution of many specialists be rationally integrated into the decision-making process; thus persuasion emerges as a key influence method. But at the same time, competitive pressures demand that these influence processes proceed quickly; that is when relationship-based power becomes important. This combination facilitates what today's environment demands—reasonably rational decision making at a moderate to fast speed.

Indirect Influence
Manipulation of the other's environment

A manager can influence someone indirectly by directly influencing others who in turn have some impact on that person.

Product manager Stein, for example, needed plant manager Billings to "sign off" on a new product idea (Product X) which Billings thought was terrible. Stein decided that there was no way he could logically persuade Billings because Billings just would not listen to him. With time, Stein felt, he could have broken through that barrier. But he did not have that time. Stein also realized that Billings would never, just because of some deal or favor, sign off on a product he did not believe in. Stein also felt it not worth the risk of trying to force Billings to sign off, so here is what he did:

- On Monday, Stein got Reynolds, a person Billings respected, to send Billings two market research studies that were very favorable to Product X, with a note attached saying, "Have you seen this? I found them rather surprising. I am not sure if I entirely believe them, but still. . . ."
- On Tuesday, Stein got a representative of one of the company's biggest customers to mention casually to Billings on the phone that he had heard a rumor about Product X being introduced soon and was "glad to see you guys are on your toes as usual."
- On Wednesday, Stein had two industrial engineers stand about three feet away from Billings before a meeting and talk about the favorable test results on Product X.
- On Thursday, Stein set up a meeting to talk about Product X with Billings and invited only people whom Billings liked or respected and who also felt favorably about Product X.
- On Friday, Stein went to see Billings and asked him if he was willing to sign off on Product X. He was.

This somewhat complex example contains many manipulative tactics which influential managers regularly use. For example, they structure the agenda, the attendance, and the timing of meetings to influence people. They send people written information selectively. They "stage" seemingly spontaneous discussions or events. And they use intermediaries to influence others.

This type of manipulation of the environment can influence both behavior and attitudes and can often succeed when other influence methods fail. But it has a number of serious drawbacks. It takes considerable time and energy, and it is quite risky. Many people think it is wrong to try to influence others in this way—even people who, without consciously recognizing it, use this technique themselves. If they think someone is trying (or has tried) to manipulate them, they may retaliate. Furthermore, people who gain the reputation of being manipulators seriously undermine their own capacities for developing power and for influencing others. Few people will want to identify with a manipulator. And virtually no one accepts, at face value, a manipulator's sincere attempts at persuasion. In extreme cases, a reputation as a manipulator can completely ruin a manager's career.

Restructuring the environment

A second way in which managers indirectly influence others is by making permanent changes in an environment. They change job descriptions, the formal systems that measure performance, the extrinsic incentives available, the tools, people, and other resources that the individual or group works with, the architecture, the norms or values of work groups, and so on. If the manager is successful in making the changes, and the changes have the desired effect on the individual or group, that effect will be sustained over time.

To get his product managers to pay more attention to profits and less attention to sales volume, one marketing vice president took four explicit steps over a period of three months. First, he changed the product managers' job descriptions to include primary responsibility for product-line profit. Second, he got the controller to include profit by product line in the monthly statements that went to product managers. Then he convinced the company's president to allow him to give product managers up to a 25 percent yearly bonus, depending upon their achievement of profit objectives. Finally, he spent time with the product managers individually and as a group explaining why their focus on profits was important to the company.

Most managers recognize that changes in the forces that surround a person can have great impact on that person's behavior. Unlike many of the other influence methods, this one does not require a large expenditure of limited resources or effort on an ongoing basis. Once such a change has been successfully made, it works independently of the manager.

This method of influence is used by all managers to some degree. Many, however, use it sparingly simply because they do not have the power to change the forces acting on the person they wish to influence. In many organizations, only top managers have the power to change such factors as the formal measurement systems, the extrinsic incentives available, and the architecture.

Using Influence Methods Successfully

The mere existence of power does not, by itself, guarantee its effective use in pursuing some objective. A striking example of this fact can be seen in the case of an incompetent heir to a large company who is given an enormous amount of power but whose inept use of that power achieves very little.

Just as some managers are better than others in acquiring power, some are more effective than others in using it. From my own observations, influential managers seem to share four important characteristics.

1. They are sensitive to what others consider to be legitimate behavior in using power.

They recognize that most people believe that power carries with it certain obligations regarding its use. A person who gains and uses a considerable amount of power based on a professional reputation is generally expected to be an expert in certain areas. If it ever becomes publicly known that the person is clearly not an expert in those areas, such a person will probably be labeled a fraud, or untrustworthy, and not only will lose his power but will suffer in other ways too. A person with whom a number of people identify is expected to act like an ideal leader. If he clearly lets people down, he will lose that power and will suffer the indignation of his ex-followers. Many managers who have created or used power based on perceived dependence in ways that their employees have felt unfair have ended up with a unionized workforce.

2. *They have a good intuitive understanding of the various ways to use power.*

Influential managers can sense which types of power are best to use with different types of people. They recognize, for example, that professionals expect to be influenced by persuasion more than by other forms of power. They also have a grasp of all the various methods of influence and what each can accomplish, at what costs, and with what risks. (This is summarized in Figure 3.) They can recognize the specific conditions in any situation and then select an influence method that is compatible with those conditions.

3. *They tend to use all the influence methods mentioned in Figure 3.*

While they generally try to avoid those influence methods that are riskier than others and those that may have negative consequences, unlike less successful managers, they do not hesitate to use any method if it is needed. They use power in an unconflicted way. They seem to recognize, if only intuitively, that all the methods are *needed* to deal with the complex and dependent situation they are in.

4. *They use all these methods to help them manage upward, downward, and laterally.*

As we saw in Chapter 2, the complex situation managers often find themselves in includes not only relationships with subordinates but dependent relations with superiors and peers (both inside and outside the organization). Effective managers use their power to manage all these relationships. They do not just manage their subordinates; they manage their bosses, their organizational peers, and outsiders too. Although textbooks have traditionally stressed only the role of downward management, effective managers seem to recognize the importance of using power to manage upward and laterally.

5

It is difficult to describe any job and discover what it calls for in employee behavior, but unusually so for managerial jobs because they change so much from one setting to another.[1]

John Campbell, Marvin Dunnette,
Edward Lawler, and Karl Weick

Situational differences in acquiring and using power

The demands placed on managers in different types of jobs in different organizations can vary substantially. The differences, for example, between a first-level production management job in a large manufacturing company and a top-level strategic planning job in a bank probably far outweigh the similarities.

In order to understand how and why a successful manager in a specific job acquires and uses power, one needs to understand thoroughly the job itself and the demands it places on the manager. In particular, one needs to appreciate the amount of job-related dependence.

Power-Oriented Behavior and Job-Related Dependence

Managerial jobs can differ significantly in the degree and extent of the manager's dependence. You saw an example of this in

[1]*Managerial Behavior, Performance, and Effectiveness* (New York: McGraw-Hill, 1970), p. 71.

Chapter 2. Another is shown graphically in Figure 4, which displays the job-related dependence for a plant manager and a hospital manager. The plant manager in this case runs a small facility which uses easily obtainable materials and a rather simple technology to manufacture a standard product for a large, stable market. He is dependent on his subordinates, suppliers, markets, and boss. Without some cooperation from these people, the manager would not be able to accomplish his job-related objectives. Nevertheless, he is not very dependent on any single supplier, because there are many alternatives. As a result of the large and stable market, the manager is not very dependent on any single customer or group of customers. Nor is he very dependent on any single competitor or group of competitors. He is, of course, dependent on subordinates to do their jobs well. But with a simple technology and a small plant, the manager could probably replace people fairly easily and, in a crisis, personally perform most of their jobs. Because of the nature of the market and the product, he is not really dependent on other parts of the company for much cooperation, with the obvious exception of his boss.

The hospital manager described in Figure 4 is in a very different position. This head of a large, publicly owned teaching hospital is dependent upon (a) the city's mayor's office—to approve the hospital's budget, to support the hospital publicly, and to try not to make a hospital employee out of everyone the mayor owes a favor to; (b) other parts of the city bureaucracy for such services as construction; (c) a dozen unions or employee associations that can call a strike or work stoppage; (d) the civil service, which can make it easy or impossible to get adequate employees; (e) the city council, which can call hearings that take up a hospital manager's time and embarrass him; (f) two accreditation agencies, which can put the hospital out of business; (g) the state government, which

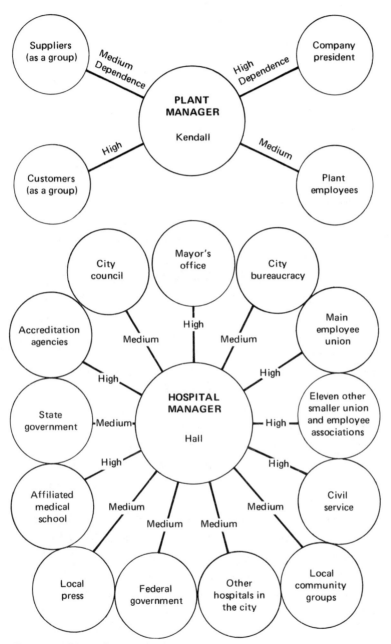

Figure 4. Dependence inherent in two managerial jobs.

can constrain hospital activities in a number of ways; (h) the medical school with which it is affiliated, which supplies the hospital with M.D.'s (i) the local press, which can embarrass the hospital and upset the mayor; (j) the federal government, which supplies the hospital with some funds and regulates some activities; (k) other hospitals in the city, whose major actions can have a positive or negative impact on this hospital; (l) the local community, which, if organized, can constrain the hospital's actions through the press, mayor, or city council; (m) and a few others still.

In studying hospital manager Hall and plant manager Kendall, I found they used the methods described in this book both to establish some countervailing power over those they were dependent upon and to make sure those people cooperated. But while hospital manager Hall spent close to 80 to 90 percent of his day acquiring and maintaining power, or influencing others, plant manager Kendall spent only 25 to 30 percent of his time involved in those activities. Kendall spent the remainder of his time performing a wide variety of other tasks that were less directly related to the acquisition and use of power: he examined and sometimes changed the daily, weekly, and monthly production plans; he talked to equipment salesmen; he answered questions from his maintenance foreman about technically difficult problems.

I have found this very important pattern in a countless number of managerial jobs: *The greater the amount of job-related dependence, the more time and energy the manager tends to put into power-oriented behavior in order to cope with that dependence.* Managing additional dependence seems to demand that additional power be acquired and used. But the acquisition and use of power is time-consuming. Therefore, as job-related dependence increases, the amount of time and energy successful managers invest in effective power-oriented behavior also tends to increase.

Furthermore, the *type* of power-oriented behavior seems to vary systematically with job-related dependence. For example, while hospital manager Hall developed and used all the types of power and methods of influence more than plant manager Kendall, the relative frequency with which he used some of the methods was also greater. Kendall rarely tried to develop power by acquiring certain resources, such as a big office, or by actively doing non-work-related favors for people, or by consciously projecting some image of himself. He also seldom tried to influence people by coercively exercising power based on perceived dependence or by elaborately manipulating their environments.

Hall, on the other hand, relied on these less socially accepted and riskier methods much more frequently. In the course of a typical week, for example, Hall may well have influenced people by means of persuasion twice as often as Kendall, while influencing people by coercion ten times as often. Likewise, he may well have spent twice as much time trying to develop a good professional reputation, while spending fifteen times as much energy developing a sense of obligation in others by doing them personal favors.

This pattern is found in many managerial jobs, in a wide diversity of settings. Specifically, *as job-related dependence increases, the relative frequency with which managers engage in the more "negative" and riskier forms of power-oriented behavior tends to increase as well.*

In response to job-related dependence, managers tend to rely on the more "positive" and less risky methods of gaining power as much as possible, while relying on the other methods only when necessary. When job-related dependence is reasonably low, a manager can successfully cope with that dependence without having to resort very much to coercion, manipulation, and the like. But as job-related dependence increases, the more acceptable methods seem generally to be less able by themselves to cope with what can be a terribly complex, demanding, and difficult situation.

The following descriptions of some of the typical problems Hall and Kendall face clearly show this pattern in the acquisition and use of power. First Kendall:

"The biggest problem I had this week was due to an equipment failure. But we handled that pretty well, I thought. As soon as a maintenance foreman decided that he just could not fix it unless he did X, Y, and Z, which would have taken two weeks, I was notified. I took a quick look at the machine myself, talked to the maintenance foreman, and then called a meeting of my purchasing and inventory manager, my scheduling manager, two maintenance people, and myself. In just one half hour we identified a number of additional ways of dealing with this problem, and then the broader implications of each alternative. I picked out what appeared to be the best choice, and the others agreed. Then I drew up a list of what had to be done, by whom, and when, and got copies for each of us. Eighteen hours later the machine was in full operation once again.

"When I first took over this job, that series of events would not have occurred. We would have solved the problem much less effectively and much more slowly. I have worked since then to get a team of supervisors underneath me who respect my manufacturing judgment, who look up to me as a good manager, and who clearly see me as the legitimate boss around here. Rational problem solving is now relatively easy."

Contrast this typical problem and how Kendall handled it with Hall's situation:

"Typical problems? Well, let me just describe this morning. On the way from the parking lot to my office I was approached by the head of one of our nonunion employee associations. He obviously had been waiting for me. He asked me what the hospital was going to do about the 'deplorable conditions' in one of the older buildings. I explained to him that the question of refurbishing parts of that building would be coming up at this month's budget meeting, and that I for one would push for asking for about $25,000 for the job. His voice level increased at this point, and he said that he really did not want to wait another six months without those 'conditions' corrected. And then he started making vague threats about leaking something to the newspapers.

"Now all this is happening while we are walking. And at that point we were inside the main building and about ten yards from my office. So I just kept on walking and didn't say anything. And he followed me right into my office. I calmly took off my coat, and then turned around and walked toward him while giving him a very cold stare. He was standing near my office door which was open, so I walked up to within a foot of him, looking him straight in the eye, and with my left hand I slammed the office door shut. It's a big door. It made a lot of noise. He jumped about a half inch off the ground. I didn't flinch. I then started to talk in a slow and very forceful voice. I listed about 20 problems that the hospital faces right now. I did this while pointing toward my desk, which has about eight years' worth of reading stacked on it. I made it perfectly clear how committed I was to dealing with these as fast and as effectively as possible. And then I . . . well, let's just say I made a very clear threat which made his earlier vague threat look pretty small. He just stood there with his mouth open.

"I went over to the intercom and asked my secretary to read my schedule for the day. Then I walked back to him, put my hand on his shoulder, stopped the cold stare, and said something like 'Look, we both care a lot about this place and our people. With the budget we have, it's enough to drive anyone crazy at times. Let's keep our heads. I'll do the best I can on it.' I then told him that I would appreciate it if he would explain to his people what my situation was and what we were trying to do about the building problem. I also pointed out that if he or they could identify any new funding sources that could pay for such rehab work, I would have my financial people file proposals for those funds. He nodded his head and looked a bit embarrassed. He said something about being sorry for the newspaper remarks, and I told him not to worry about it. He left my office with a handshake, while promising to talk to his people.

"I had one other highlight in my morning. We had a meeting at 11:00 regarding a new piece of equipment one of our labs is trying to get. The problem here is that to buy this instrument, we need to get an endless number of people to sign off first. And before anyone will sign, they always want something in return. It's incredible. The state department of health, for example, wants us to add one new type of patient care service, while dropping two other types. Well, anyway, this must be our twentieth meeting on the problem, and each time after about 15 minutes the head of the lab that wants the instrument goes into hysterics about the lost opportunity for research and better patient care. So we have to pause and calm him down. Today's meeting ended as usual with promises from everyone to do certain things over the next two weeks. But a lot of this burden falls on me. I agreed, for example, to try to make a deal with HEW so that they will sign off on this. And I agreed to twist a few arms inside the hospital to get all our internal sign-offs cleared.

"Some days are much calmer than today. Some days are much worse."

The relationship of power-oriented behavior to job-related dependence is terribly important because many managers do not seem to be aware of how much the amount and type of power-oriented behavior need to vary in different settings. And that lack of understanding can create serious career problems for them, especially when they accept a new job or a promotion into a position that seems similar to previous jobs but that has significantly more job-related dependence.

I will have much more to say about these career issues in Chapter 7. But first, we need to further explore the critical situational variable that links power-oriented behavior and managerial career success.

Variation in Job-Related Dependence

The pattern of dependence inherent in managerial jobs varies within an organization and across organizations in reasonably predictable ways. A number of factors seem to be closely related to that variation.

Within an organization

Within an organization, the amount of dependence in jobs tends to be related closely to four factors:

1. *Job responsibilities.* The more responsibilities inherent in the job, the more the incumbent is forced to rely on others to perform tasks and cooperate, and thus the greater the dependence.

2. *Direct and indirect reports.* The more people who report directly and indirectly to a managerial position, and the greater the difficulty of replacing those people or doing their jobs, the greater the position-related dependence.

3. *Self-containment.* The less a managerial job is designed to focus on self-contained tasks, the more the job is interdependent with other jobs and departments, and thus the greater the job-related dependence.

4. *Bosses.* The more higher-level positions that have some authority over a managerial job, the greater the dependence in that job.

Because of factors 1 and 2, as one moves up the management hierarchy dependence tends to increase. A top-level manager in an organization can be moderately or highly dependent on subordinates, subordinates of subordinates, peers, outside suppliers or customers, and still others. Because of the third factor, however, a lower-level job that has few if any people reporting to it can still have considerable dependence. For example, if a first-level manager is in a coordinating role, he could become moderately dependent on all those whom he must coordinate. At the extreme, this could involve over a dozen people or departments. And because of the fourth factor, it is possible for upper middle-management jobs to contain as much or more dependence than top management jobs. Upper middle-level managers often have subordinates, subordinates of subordinates, peers, and outsiders to worry about—much like the top managers. But unlike the top group, they also have a group of supervisors that they must depend upon.

Because of factors 1 and 2, line managerial jobs tend to have more dependence associated with them than staff jobs. Unlike a staff manager, a line manager often has bottom-line responsibilities which make him dependent on many others, sometimes including hundreds or thousands of subordinates.

Across organizations

Job-related dependence can also vary a great deal between similar positions in different organizations. In Hall's hospital, for example, the average managerial job would contain considerably more dependence than the average managerial job in Kendall's plant. From my own observations, I would say the following factors relate to the average amount of dependence in all managerial jobs in an organization.

1. *Organizational size.* Generally, the larger the organization, the greater the division of labor and thus the more the average managerial job must depend upon other specialties and support services.

2. *Environmental dependences.* An organization's dependence

on unions, suppliers, regulators, buyers, and competitors gets passed on to its managers, who must cope with them. The greater the amount of this environmental dependence, the larger the average dependence in managerial jobs.

3. *Environmental uncertainty*. The more uncertain the organization's environment, the less managers can make accurate assumptions about the environment (which are based on historical patterns) and thus the more they must depend on others—especially those who are monitoring the environment.

4. *Organizational goals*. The more ambitious an organization's goals, the more efficiently it must coordinate its actions to accomplish those goals. Higher coordination standards, in turn, increase the interdependence of the various parts of the organization and, with it, the average dependence in managerial jobs.

5. *Resource scarcity*. The scarcer an organization's resources (due to lack of growth or profitability or adequate funding) the more managers are forced to compete with each other for available resources and thus the more dependent they are on each other.

6. *Technology*. The more complex and sophisticated the technology employed by an organization, the greater the division of labor and specialization, which produces a greater need for coordination of those specialists. The increased coordination needs will, of course, increase the average dependence in managerial jobs.

7. *Physical proximity of operations*. The more an organization is dispersed geographically, the more independently the managers in remote units will be able to act. Conversely, the more geographically consolidated an organization is, the more dependence exists in many managerial jobs.

8. *Formal structure*. The more diffused the formal authority in the organization, the more managers tend to be dependent on managers other than their boss(es).

9. *Performance Measurement.* The more an organization's measurement systems clearly and unquestionably measure the individual performance of managers, the less those managers will be dependent on others for their pay and promotions.

10. *Reward systems.* The more the formal reward system rewards group rather than individual effort, the more dependence will surface in managerial jobs.

Because of factors 1, 2, 3, 5, 8, 9, and 10, managers in public organizations tend to be more dependent than managers in private organizations. Because of factors 2, 3, 6, 8, and 9, managers in more complex industries tend to be in a more dependent position than managers in less complex industries.

These factors provide an important understanding of job-related dependence, whose relationship to power-oriented behavior has been discussed earlier. This understanding helps one to predict, without having to do a detailed analysis of specific jobs, how much power-oriented behavior managers in different settings will probably engage in. For example, an understanding of these factors would lead us to predict, without much careful examination of the jobs involved, that Kendall would engage in significantly less power-oriented behavior than Hall. (Kendall manages a much smaller group of people; few of them are difficult to replace or perform jobs that Kendall could not. In addition, the plant operates in a more stable environment, is smaller and not very dependent on any external element except corporate headquarters, uses a simpler technology, has more centralized power, and has more elaborate quantitative systems to measure managerial performance. These factors all suggest that Kendall has less job-related dependence than Hall.)

In addition, an understanding of these factors can help one see why two seemingly identical jobs—such as two plant manager positions—can be very different. Kendall's job, for example, would be very different if it were in a much larger

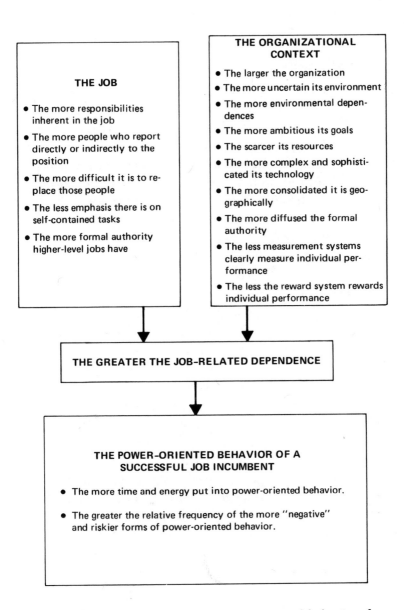

Figure 5. Relationship between the power-oriented behavior of an effective manager and key situational contingencies.

organization which faced more environmental uncertainty and dependence or which used a more complex technology.

Other contingencies

The most important factor associated with situational differences in how managers acquire and use power is job-related dependence. (See Figure 5.) But this is not the only contingency. A number of other factors are also relevant, such as the manager's style, the type of people upon whom the manager is dependent, the kind of resources available in the organization, and the climate or tone set by top management. The way in which these additional factors affect power-oriented behavior is fairly obvious. For example, if the manager has a rather uncharismatic personality, he will probably not try to develop much power over others through their identification with him. If the manager is surrounded by highly educated people who respect knowledge and expertise, he will probably rely heavily on his professional reputation and on persuasion. If the manager's organization has an overabundance of office space, he will not try to rely on his control of office space to develop the power of perceived dependence.

Perhaps the most important of these other factors, in some ways the most subtle, is the manager's bosses. They can directly influence power-oriented behavior by rewarding or punishing certain actions. They can indirectly affect such behavior by manipulating factors that shape job-related dependence (as in Figure 5). Their actions in this regard can help managers and their organizations be more effective, or their actions can create serious problems—as we shall see in the next chapter.

6

The misuse of power

The basic relationship between effective management and power-oriented behavior can be summarized as such: With greater job-related dependence, the need for power-oriented behavior—and its riskier forms—increases. In managerial jobs that have relatively little dependence, a person can be somewhat unskilled at or unwilling to engage in power-oriented behavior and still be reasonably effective. In such jobs a person could well be effective primarily because of intelligence, motivation, and expertise in the organization's technology, product, or markets. However, in managerial jobs that have a great deal of dependence, it is virtually impossible to be effective without engaging considerably in power-oriented behavior. In other words, in most managerial jobs an inability or unwillingness to acquire and use power results in ineffective performance. Dependence does not get managed, and inevitably under those circumstances, some activities will not be accomplished or will not be achieved efficiently.

Nevertheless, power-oriented behavior alone does not guarantee good performance, for two reasons: first, because other types of behavior are obviously also needed in most management jobs (such as technical competence at market research); and second, because power-oriented behavior which manages job-related dependence adequately can still have a negative impact on other individuals or activities, thus hurting the organization more than it helps.

In the previous chapters I have consistently ducked the issue of power misuse—that is, the use of power in ways that might help an individual manager but hurt the organization. In this chapter I will stop ducking.

Examples of the Misuse of Power

Some managers achieve their objectives, but at a cost to the organization much greater than the benefit. They achieve their individual goals but leave a wake of destruction in their path. One manager in a large conglomerate, for example, is alleged by many of his former subordinates to have been responsible for the virtual collapse of their division. Walt Sofer, the manager in this case, was head of that division for two years before he was promoted to a corporate position. Since he has left, the division's performance has gone down considerably. Sofer's former subordinates, most of whom now work for other companies, trace the decline to decisions he made and often forcibly implemented in the areas of personnel and resource allocation. For example, to boost divisional profits during the two years he headed the division, Sofer severely cut equipment maintenance budgets and management training budgets. When two of the divisions' best managers balked at this resource allocation decision, he fired them.

Other managers will occasionally reduce their job-related dependence to a bare minimum so they can more easily manage it, regardless of the negative organizational consequences. George Miller is a good example. He was named president of the manufacturing division of Folsum Industries when John Folsum, the founder of the company, retired. Folsum was childless and, according to his friends, looked upon Miller as a son. After being in the job for a year or so Miller reorganized the top levels of the division. Instead of having 6 vice presidents report to him, Miller had no less than 22 people report to him, most of them subordinate to his vice presidents. Although this move eventually created organizational chaos, it helped him avoid being highly dependent on his two key vice presidents (marketing and manufacturing). A second way in which he responded to the situation was, in effect, to abandon any growth and profitability goals for the division, thus implicitly setting his target at maintaining the status quo, despite the fact that the division was almost losing money. In these and other ways he reduced his job-related dependence to the point where he could just about manage it.

Other managers misuse their power by building and protecting little kingdoms within their organizations. In one company, for example, the sales force was nearly twice as large, per dollar of sales, as any other sales force in their industry. The crippling drain it placed on corporate resources was obvious to everyone, yet the sales vice president had been successful for years in defending his domain against budget cuts.

In smaller and more subtle ways, probably a large number of managers engage in some power-oriented behavior that is not in their organization's best interests. Division managers, for example, will sometimes hire staff specialists to work for them so that they do not have to depend on the same type of specialists on the corporate staff. These decisions can cost the companies involved from $40,000 to $250,000 per year and yet benefit them very little. Middle managers will sometimes develop the habit of always arriving late to meetings with their subordinates, thus continuously wasting their time. Still other managers will allow their subordinates to do personal errands for them when they should be working. And first-line managers, especially those supervising routine functions, will sometimes selectively enforce or ignore work rules in order to gain power over others, regardless of the negative organizational consequences.

You have undoubtedly seen a number of such examples of power misuse yourself. Clearly, that power is occasionally misused by managers is not a question. The relevant question is *why*. Why is it that some successful managers use power in ways that undermine organizational effectiveness, while others do not?

Personal Integrity

Discussions of power misuse tend to focus on an individual's values and moral beliefs. Differences in behavior and outcome are often attributed to differences in individual scruples. Many believe that if a person has values and motives which are oriented toward the greater "good," he or she is less likely to misuse power for personal gain at the cost of negative organizational or social outcomes.

Considerable evidence exists supporting the view that the values, moral beliefs, and other personality characteristics that individual managers bring to an organization are important factors in linking power-oriented behavior and organizational effectiveness. David McClelland, for example, has found that good managers have a strong power motivation, but one that is oriented toward serving the institution, not toward personal aggrandizement.[1] We have all recently seen examples in the public arena where "blind ambition," a drive only for personal success, contributed to a misuse of power.

A recognition of these and other facts has led many organizations for years to stress integrity in hiring and promoting managers. While some managers and organizations probably

[1] See David McClelland and David Burnham, "Power Is the Great Motivator," *Harvard Business Review*, March–April 1976, pp. 100–110.

underestimate the importance of personal integrity, others may overestimate its importance. Or rather, they underestimate or overlook the fact that other factors besides a lack of integrity can also lead to the misuse of power. I would say that those other factors might even be more central to power misuse than personal integrity.

Mismatch Between Job Dependence and Power Skills

In some situations, I have found relatively successful managers of moderate to high integrity in jobs that demand power skills that they just did not have. In their attempts to cope with the situation without "failing," they ended up engaging in power-oriented behavior that had negative organizational consequences. In other instances where successful managers misused power, they were in essentially unmanageable situations. Their job made them so dependent on so many people that even a person with extraordinary power skills would have had difficulty performing well. In these cases the incumbents coped by focusing on that dependence most relevant to their career success, and not even trying to manage some of the dependence that was relevant to the organization's effectiveness. Again, even people of moderate to high integrity behaved this way. In other words, *the misuse of power often seems to occur when the dependence inherent in a managerial job is significantly greater than the power skills of the job incumbent, even though the incumbent has previously displayed a moderately high level of personal integrity.*

The case of George Miller, the president of the manufacturing division described earlier, fits this pattern. Miller had displayed integrity throughout his career. But after his promotion to the presidency of a division, he clearly engaged in power-oriented behavior that hurt the division. And it seems just as clear that he did so in order to cope with a situation that was over his head. He did not have the power skills needed to effectively manage the dependence inherent in that job. So in his efforts to cope, to stay afloat, he resorted to tactics that others would label a misuse of power.

The first-line supervisor or foreman who misuses power often fits this pattern. Such people are usually either new college-educated employees or older individuals promoted from the worker ranks. In either case, they often have not had the opportunity to develop sophisticated power skills. Yet they are often put into moderately high dependence jobs and given few resources or opportunities to develop countervailing power. To cope with this situation, even people of integrity sometimes end up behaving in ways that involve power misuse.

Middle-level managers who misuse power by jealously refusing to help up-and-coming younger managers, or by arriving late at meetings just to remind their subordinates "who is boss," also fit this pattern. They are people who, from the point of view of power skills, are in jobs they cannot handle. Often because they do not see other options for their careers, they cling to their current jobs, misusing power in the process.

The case of Walt Sofer, who was promoted to a corporate vice president, also fits this pattern, but in a different way. Sofer was a very skilled person who was not over his head in his job. Everything worked well for him until the chairman and president of his conglomerate put him under enormous pressure to increase short-run earnings. They also made it clear, without saying anything directly, that they were not concerned about other consequences. Meeting their demands without misusing power quite probably was impossible in Sofer's situation. Of course he could have resigned instead of "sacrificing his integrity." But in this type of situation, it is very easy for a person like Sofer to convince himself that in not resigning he is really taking the right step for himself and his organization.

A similar case, involving Ron Kaplan, more clearly shows how a person with integrity can misuse power instead of resigning. Kaplan was the manager of an East Coast office in a moderately large service organization. He had known little besides success. He had always done well in school. Since graduating from business school he had received some type of promotion every two years. Just after his thirty-fourth birthday he was put in charge of his company's fourth largest office. His family and friends expected him to continue to be successful. So did Kaplan.

In June of 1973 Kaplan had a meeting with his firm's chairman in which the chairman stressed the importance of not losing a particular client. At the time, Kaplan thought this meeting was rather odd since that client accounted for only one half of one percent of the firm's business. He soon forgot about this meeting. Later, in September, he received the smallest yearly bonus he had ever received since joining the firm. At first, he thought it was obviously a mistake; in the previous year his office had increased its sales by 15 percent and its profits by 18 percent at the same time that it upgraded some of its staff and added a new type of service. He subsequently found out from the firm's president that it was not a mistake—top management was disappointed that its expressed concern for a certain client had not been satisfactorily dealt with. The client was close to dropping relations with the firm.

Kaplan attempted to explain what was so obvious to him: that the client was not so important to the company and that meeting management demands would cost his office much more than it would benefit the firm. The president made it very clear that he was not interested in listening to Kaplan. Instead, he was interested in the chairman's desire that they keep the client.

Kaplan immediately thought about resigning. But the more he thought about it, the less attractive that alternative looked. He kept thinking of troublesome questions. How was he going to explain his resignation to others? And what would his current supervisors say when a new potential employer approached them? If the situation got ugly, what impact would that have on his career? And what impact would that have on the family that depended on him? He then began to worry that maybe the chairman had information he did not have about the importance of that one client to the firm. Was he just being stubborn, insensitive, and disloyal? What harm would it do to be sensitive to his superior's desires? Didn't he ask his employees, under some circumstances, to do things that did not make sense to them? He had his orders in this case. Why was he waiting?

In October 1974, Ron Kaplan began to implement a series of decisions that shifted his and his staff's attention away from a number of clients and toward that one client. He always tried to find ways to do this so that other aspects of organizational effectiveness were not undermined. But in many cases this was not possible. For example, he dropped three projects aimed at staff training because he was too busy. He allocated an unusually large budget for "entertainment" for the client. When one of his staff began to seriously question these moves, he had him transferred. Kaplan rationalized his actions as doing what was best for the firm.

George Miller's boss, the president of Folsum Industries, was in much the same situation. He was under considerable pressure from the retired founder, who still owned 60 percent of the stock, to allow Miller to do what he wanted, and not to remove him from his job. Miller's boss tried to find ways to cope with the founder without allowing Miller's division to deteriorate. But he was largely unsuccessful. So he chose to use his power to placate the founder and to allow Miller to stay. He justified this decision in his own mind by thinking that if he left, Miller would probably be promoted to replace him, and that would undermine the company's effectiveness even more.

If men of higher integrity had been confronted with Miller's situation, or his boss's, or Kaplan's, they might have reacted differently. They might have resigned, or confronted their supervisors more forcefully. But one cannot help wonder if many managers really would have behaved differently, especially in light of how our society treats "failures."

The Critical Impact of Top Management

The cases of Miller, Kaplan, and Sofer all highlight another important pattern related to power misuse. *Many cases of power misuse at middle and lower management levels can be traced to other cases of power misuse at the very top of the organizations involved.* It was the top management in Miller's, Kaplan's, and Sofer's organizations that created the situations these men found themselves in. Specifically, those top managers used their power to make staffing decisions, or to manipulate the dependence inherent in jobs below them so that a significant gap emerged between the lower-level manager's power skills and his dependence. This behavior on the part of top management then directly led to the episodes of power misuse below them.

Top managers seem to misuse their power and generate power misuse below them for reasons that are very similar to those found in the cases of middle- and lower-level managers. That is, they do so when they do not have the power skills to manage the dependence inherent in their jobs, or when their job-related dependence is virtually impossible to manage. Personal integrity is a relevant factor in helping us to understand these situations, but it is not sufficient by itself.

Walt Sofer's bosses were under enormous pressure from the financial community, both directly and through their board of directors, to increase short-term earnings. Their efforts to manage their dependence without putting dysfunctional pressure on their divisional managers were unsuccessful. So they began pressuring these managers. A different set of people might have been more successful at generating power-oriented behavior that could cope with this situation without the dysfunctional consequences. It is hard to be sure. It is also not clear that their firm would have been better off if they resigned to "preserve their integrity."

The chairman of the board in Ron Kaplan's firm was 72 years old. He had delayed his retirement twice before, at ages 65 and 70. Several members of his board of directors were putting pressure on him to retire because they felt he was not effective in his job. In his efforts to cope with his dependence on the board, the chairman pointed out that the firm had held five clients successfully for over 20 years each, an unusual situation in their industry. When he later heard that one of those five clients might soon sever relations with his firm, he set into motion the scenario that led to Ron Kaplan's misuse of power.

Under these circumstances, the burden for creating organizational effectiveness and minimizing power misuse falls heavily on top managers. They must use their power to establish and maintain a framework in which those who are hired and promoted have both integrity *and* the power skills necessary for the job. They must see to it that the organization's formal structure and reward systems, as well as its informal culture and social structure, reinforce those actions. In most organizations this is a difficult task, requiring extraordinarily talented and dedicated people. But in some organizations it may well be an impossible task.

Impossible Situations

Some organizations score highly on all the factors associated with a high level of dependence in managerial jobs. In these organizations, the dependence in the top jobs can be extremely high—quite possibly too large for any individual to handle without resorting to power misuse. In these situations, one typically finds a top manager who is not really in control of the organization. Political behavior and power misuse occur throughout the organization. Little coordinated planning is done. Organizational arrangements come to reflect internal power balances much more than they do business or environmental realities. As a result of all these factors, the organization performs poorly.

Not many organizations fit this pattern today, but perhaps this may change in the future. Many trends today are either increasing the dependence in managerial jobs or making it more difficult for managers to establish countervailing power. Increasing governmental intervention, increasing organizational size, and decreasing respect for authority are just a few. If these trends continue, many more organizations may become less manageable, more political, and less effective.[2] Somehow I do not think we are at all prepared for such an eventuality.

My objective in this chapter has not been to minimize the importance of personal integrity. To the contrary, integrity clearly is an important factor that links power-oriented behavior and organizational effectiveness. I have only been suggesting that two other factors, which are often overlooked, are just as important. The first factor is job-related dependence. The second is power skills and abilities. (See Figure 6.)

Whenever a significant gap exists between the dependence inherent in a managerial job and the power skills of the job incumbent, some organizational ineffectiveness seems to be inevitable. In some instances, the ineffectiveness results without power misuse; the incumbent is simply not able to manage the job dependence, does not accomplish his job-related objectives, is not effective in his job, and thus does not contribute to organizational effectiveness. In such cases the manager is

---

[2] This possibility is very troubling. I have not explored it in more depth here, despite its potential importance, simply because it is beyond the scope of this book.

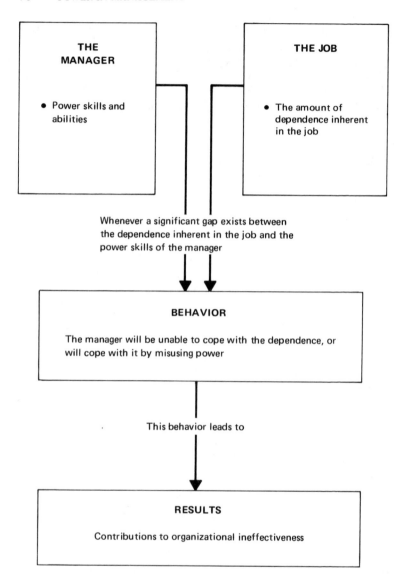

Figure 6. Power skills and organizational effectiveness.

usually transferred, demoted, or fired. In other situations, the incumbent essentially misuses power in order to cope with the dependence that is most relevant to career success. Such a person will not accomplish all job-related objectives, but he often will at least survive. In some cases, even individuals who have a history of integrity will behave this way.

A number of factors often help create situations in which a significant gap develops between a manager's power skills and his or her dependence. Poor judgment on the part of individuals making or accepting hiring and promotion decisions is sometimes to blame. So is poor judgment about the amount of dependence designed into jobs. A lack of integrity in those making any of these decisions can also be a contributing factor, as can a changing situation which suddenly increases and complicates the dependence.

The negative consequences of a large gap between job dependence and power skills usually become more significant as one goes up the hierarchy in an organization. Such a gap typically creates similar gaps in lower-level jobs in the same reporting hierarchy. Thus the burden for creating organizational effectiveness and minimizing power misuse falls heavily on top managers—perhaps too heavily at times for even the most talented people.

7

Power-oriented behavior and success in managerial careers

Managers who have little skill at or inclination toward power-oriented behavior sometimes remain in low-level managerial jobs throughout their careers, with few subordinates and few coordination responsibilities. Occasionally they are demoted into such jobs after it becomes clear that they cannot or will not manage the larger dependence in higher-level managerial jobs. Or they move to an organization where most managerial jobs have very little dependence. Most often, however, especially if they are well educated, these people move into more specialized professional roles. Jobs such as a senior scientist, corporate compensation specialist, and chief financial analyst allow them to be more independent.

On the other hand, people who have power-oriented inclinations and skills are usually successful in managerial careers. Because job dependence tends to increase with the level of hierarchy, the greater a person's power skills and inclinations, the further he or she tends to rise in that hierarchy (all other individual factors being equal). If such a person seriously *lacks* one or more of the other personal characteristics that managerial jobs often demand (such as a willingness to work fairly long hours and a certain minimum intelligence) he or she will, of course, have a lackluster career in management and will often be labeled a "politician."

Managers who have the skill and inclination for power-oriented behavior—indeed for more than their jobs demand—often rise rapidly in organizations. They do so by expanding the dependence in their jobs. One young star in a large multinational organization always took on two or three large and important projects above his regular managerial duties. Each project, of course, brought with it more dependence. By heading a task force to explore locations for a new plant site, for instance, be became dependent on all members of the task force—none of whom he normally interacted with. Nevertheless, his capacity for engaging effectively in power-oriented behavior, along with his other skills, allowed him to manage all that dependence and to accomplish the objectives of his regular job and his extra projects. That performance, in turn, led to a series of quick promotions for him. This career pattern is typical for many "fast track" people, and it continues until they reach a level where the regular job dependence is all they can handle.

Typical Career Problems

People who have power-oriented skills tend to be successful in managerial careers as long as they have other necessary managerial qualifications. Nevertheless, many of these people experience problems at one point or another in their careers: problems usually associated either with a mismatch between their skills and abilities and the requirements of a job they accepted or with adaptation to a new job. Many of these problems could probably be avoided if they had a better understanding of power dynamics in management.

Mismatch between individual and job

A mismatch between an individual's basic skills and abilities and the requirements of a managerial job inevitably leads to poor performance. If the mismatch is large, the poor performance is usually followed by a resignation, a termination, a transfer, or a demotion. Before accepting a new job, managers seem always to assess even if only intuitively whether such a mismatch exists or not. But sometimes they make poor conscious or unconscious assessments because of a lack of familiarity with the issues discussed in this book.

Take, for example, the case of a vice president of an enormously successful corporation who had a brilliant career with that company. At age 46, it became clear to him that the current president would not retire for at least ten more years. He decided he did not want to wait and was getting just a little bored with the company and products that had occupied his mind for 20 years. When offered the presidency of an innovative, prestigious, nonprofit corporation, he accepted. In the first month of his new job, he initiated a number of organizational changes aimed at rationalizing some arrangements that were more historical accident than design. At one point he ran into resistance from a middle-level employee who seemed to be untalented and disruptive. He fired him. When news of the firing reached the other employees, pandemonium erupted. The work of the organization almost stopped completely. Friends of the employee staged a sit-in strike in the president's office. Other groups of employees started a drive to form a union. Four days later, while things were still in an uproar, the president resigned.

In this case, the highly successful manager took a new

position whose job-related dependence was very different from his old job. In his new role, he was much more dependent on his employees—for a variety of reasons related to the organization's structure, technology, and markets. He apparently started in his new role without an appreciation for this change in dependence. When the blowup occurred, he found that having to deal with that dependence—having to spend considerable time being sensitive to it, reducing it, gaining countervailing power, and influencing others—was "an unbelievably frustrating waste of my time."

This reaction is typical of a person who is in a job that calls for more power-oriented behavior than he or she can or wants to offer. Such people often label the needed behavior "a waste of time," "silly politics," and the like.

Less dramatic examples of job–individual mismatches are more common. A person accepts a job and finds that because of either training or lack of intelligence he or she does not understand many of the issues or problems involved. Such a person finds himself unable to develop much power through information or to influence people significantly through persuasion. Sometimes the person then simply fails to cope with job-related dependence and is removed. In other cases the person tries to compensate by developing still more resource or relationship power and by trying to influence people through means other than persuasion. Such a person may survive in the job, at least for a while. But even then he or she typically is labeled a "politician" and achieves no further career success.

Adaptation problems

A manager whose power skills fit a new job will still often have some difficulty adapting to the job demands. Unrealistic beliefs about power dynamics in management cause a significant number of these adaptation problems.

For example, people in their first management jobs will often display an insensitivity to job-related dependence that gets them into trouble. Because they are seldom if ever told in their formal education that they need to identify those they depend on, even people who are naturally sensitive to social phenomena can experience some problems.

"When I started work at Balor Chemical," one such person reported, "the very first day I got my hands on an organization chart and picture book [a pamphlet with pictures and short biographies of the company's management] and started learning who was who. I thought I was pretty smart; and I was, compared with the other people who also started work at about the same time. After two weeks I knew my way around—who to call for what, how to get things done—better than most of them did after two months. In retrospect, after one and a half years on the job, it is hard to believe how little I really did know. For example, Helen Wagner wasn't in any picture book or on any organization chart, but she is about as important as anyone to the success of the acquisition that I'm working on now. Helen is [executive vice president] Phil Peters' secretary. Phil is my boss on this project. There are a variety of key decisions that I have to clear through him that come up occasionally and demand a reasonably quick or very quick response. Phil's office is in Manhattan in our headquarters building, and so my access to him on the phone or by memo is through Helen. And as you can imagine, he is very busy and gets lots of phone calls and mail. Helen is responsible for making judgments by herself regarding priorities. She's got the power to make my life very difficult.

"Then there's Marvin Wick, whose official title is something obscure and who is buried in the corporate finance department, but who at the same time decides whose requests outside the department for routine financial staff work will be honored, and if so how quickly and with what expertise. Officially those types of requests are supposed to be directed to the department head's administrative assistant, but it's Marvin who ends up making the decisions. Every once in a while I need those services, since that is hardly my specialty. At that point Marv becomes the central person in my life. Then there's Phil Racko in legal, and Janet Rolly in ad services, and Jim Ballentine in planning, and on and on. I only wish I knew all this one year ago. I could have gotten a lot more done, and avoided a number of problems."

Unlike this one young manager, some people experience adaptation problems because they do not try to manage their job-related dependence. Because of their inaccurate notions about power, management, and organizations, they feel that they should not have to "get these other people to do their jobs," as one person put it. So they do not even try, at least at first, to obtain and use power to manage that dependence. Fred Talbor is typical in this regard. He reports: "The biggest problem I had adapting to my current job was learning how to live without my own accounting staff. In my previous job, I had a chief accountant and two clerks on my staff. In this job, I have no accounting support; I rely on the corporate accounting staff. In my previous job, I never had any problems with accounting. I got the reports when I needed them. In this job, I started having problems the first month I was here. The first report I got came about a week after I wanted it and had about half the information I needed along with lots of information I couldn't care less about. I called corporate accounting, and the war started. I got so mad at one point that I stood here in my office and screamed at my poor secretary, 'Why can't those incompetent bastards do anything right?' Well, to make a long story short, what in retrospect looks obvious finally dawned on me: I was as much a part of the problem as they were. I was not adjusting to a new set of realities in an intelligent way. Shouting was not helping. Since then I have taken the time to develop a good relationship with corporate accounting and to use that to get the kind of reports I want, when I want."

People whose dependence in their new jobs is considerably greater than in former jobs often experience problems because they fail to recognize what type of adaptation is needed. Without an understanding of the issues and patterns identified in the previous chapters, they frequently respond in what is sometimes labeled a "naive" way.

Elliot Katz, for example, was quite successful in his first managerial job. When he was promoted to a position in a much larger division of the same corporation, he was almost fired after nine months. He did quit after a year. Katz's subsequent assessment of his career problem focuses on his power naiveté:

"I recognized when I was promoted that my new job was more complex, and that it would put me in a less independent position. I could see that there were lots of people I was going to have to deal with. But I did not appreciate the implications of this difference. In my first job I didn't worry about the 'visibility' of my achievements. Had anyone suggested that I should, I would have told them I didn't have the time for that political bull. What I did not see at the time was that because of the nature of the division I was in and my job, my accomplishments were obvious to my boss and easy for him to measure. And he was the only person who really counted.

"After my promotion, my position was very different. There were lots of people who counted besides my immediate superior. Because of the nature of the situation my performance was not visible to many of them, and it was not easy for others to evaluate. Under those circumstances, I should have developed good relations with those people whose cooperation and respect I needed by taking explicit steps to make my achievements visible. I didn't realize this at the time and didn't do it. I also didn't realize that there are times when the only way you can deal with some people is by hitting them on top of the head, or bribing them to leave town. Now, I don't mean that literally of course. I just mean that there are times when rational dialog is useless. Granted, these times are relatively rare, but they can be important instances. Looking back on those events after my first promotion, I see myself as pretty naive. And I got beaten up a bit because of it."

To a lesser extent, some managers experience almost the opposite adjustment problem. Managers in their first jobs—those who, like Elliot Katz, have just suffered a career defeat and those who have just moved to a job with significantly less dependence than their previous job—sometimes treat power issues in a very cynical way. They overemphasize the importance of power-oriented behavior. And they seriously underestimate the crucial function that trust plays in dealing with people. These attitudes eventually cause them serious problems. For example, one executive reported:

"We hired a man about two years ago who left after six months, by which time he had already driven a few of us up the wall. He was obsessed with organizational politics. It was incredible. He would sit on the simplest decision for weeks while he thought out all the possible political implications. He spent time establishing and nurturing relationships with dozens of people who had nothing to do with his job. I'm not sure if I ever had a straightforward conversation with him; he was so concerned about what I thought of him. Now don't misunderstand. I'm not suggesting that developing relationships and being sensitive to power is wrong; it's just that he had things so out of proportion."

Ironically, although the naive and the cynical probably see themselves as at opposite ends of a continuum, they often suffer very similar problems in adapting to new positions and in other aspects of their careers. The one characteristic they have in common—the lack of realistic understanding of power—proves to be more important than their differences.

Overcoming and Avoiding Career Problems

The typical career problems managers encounter through lack of understanding of power dynamics can be overcome or completely avoided by most people. The key is awareness—that is, a familiarity with the issues discussed in this book. A few examples will help clarify this point.

Choosing a job

An awareness of power/dependence patterns helped a very successful 35-year-old manager decide whether to accept an offer to take over as the head of a division in another company. This offer was, on the surface at least, a great opportunity for him. Most of his colleagues assumed he would immediately accept the offer. Yet he had reservations that he just could not articulate. Exposure to the previous material in this book helped him to identify consciously the source of those reservations. It seems that the new job would have required considerably more power-oriented behavior than his current job, and yet there was little evidence that he could generate and maintain that type of behavior effectively. He already, for example, felt strongly that he was spending too much time attending meetings and talking to people. Before the exposure, he had tentatively decided to take the job, despite his feelings, because it looked like the rational thing to do. But with his new awareness, he turned it down.

An understanding of power dynamics has helped a number of my students in a similar way during their search for jobs. Each year there are always some students who know from prior experience that they do not function well in highly political environments. Most initially assume that the only way they can find out whether a potential job is in a highly political environment is to talk to someone who is closely acquainted with the job and the organization, or to visit the place themselves. The material in Chapter 5 gives them a practical alternative. It says that highly political environments will be found in organizations that have a high level of dependence in managerial jobs. It also suggests that those organizations will be characterized by such factors as (a) large size, (b) high environmental uncertainty, (c) many environmental dependences, (d) ambitious organizational goals, (e) complex technologies, (f) diffused formal authority, and (g) scarce resources. By screening out organizations that have many of these characteristics, these students have become much more efficient in their search for jobs.

Adapting to a job

An understanding of power dynamics can also help managers adapt to a new job. In one instance, it helped a young, professionally trained manager identify why he was having difficulties in a new job. Specifically, it clearly highlighted the fact that he was not managing (by means of power-oriented behavior) his dependence on two very important people. As a result, they were periodically interfering with his work and blocking his achievements. Both people were in a different department that controlled resources important to his projects. He was apparently not aware of just how dependent he was on these two people, especially since that dependence was not shown on any organization chart or in a job description. Although he had recognized them as sources of annoyance, he had previously defined the problem as theirs, not his. As he put it, "I just thought to myself—they shouldn't behave that way!" Through his new awareness he was able to identify some ways in which he could alter his own behavior in order to develop, maintain, and use power to influence those two people. He learned, for example, that one of them loved to play squash but had difficulty finding partners. Since our young manager played regularly too, he decided to ask this person to play squash with him. He reasoned that a periodic squash match would (a) offer him the opportunity to develop at least one type of power over the other person—power based on a perceived obligation to return favors; (b) provide a source of up-to-date information on what this person was doing; (c) offer him a relaxed setting in which he could try to influence the other person when necessary; and (d) cost him none of his most valuable resource—time—because he would have played squash with someone anyway. Over a period of a month he implemented these new ideas. And within a two-month period his job performance, as both he and his boss perceived it, went up appreciably.

Making decisions on personnel and organization design

An understanding of power dynamics can also assist managers in making a variety of personnel and organizational decisions. I used the material in this book, for example, to help a client who had tentatively decided to fire an important middle-level manager. My client was upset because this individual was behaving in "very political ways that are hurting the company." Among other things, the subordinate was using his power skills to get a higher priority from the data-processing facility than was in the best interests of the company; more important projects were being bumped for his. My analysis suggested that this manager was simply trying to cope with the dependence framework that was imposed on him largely by his boss and my client. Needless to say, my client was less than enthusiastic about the results of my analysis. Nevertheless, it did stop him from firing the other manager and eventually led him to review his top-level organization and his own leadership style.

A number of managers have used a similar form of analysis to help them make hiring and promotion decisions. In these cases, they use their insights in a manner similar to the way job choosers use it: to help them assess how well the person fits the job. One vice president in a publishing company was interested in filling an important job that reported to him. One of the applicants for the job really intrigued the vice president. He was an unusually bright and affable young man. But he had no experience in publishing or in the kind of job being filled. In looking for different ways to assess whether this young man could fit the job opening, the vice president used the material in this book. Specifically, he assessed the positions the young man had been successful in and compared them with the job opening in terms of job-related dependences. In doing so, he concluded that they were very similar. Based on that insight and other types of analyses, he hired the young man. As of this date, the decision appears to have been a very good one.

Understanding the behavior of others

A familiarity with power dynamics can help managers understand the behavior of key people with whom they interact. One manager in a university setting, for example, was unable to understand certain aspects of the university president's behavior in his relations with the trustees. This lack of understanding led to the first negative interaction he had had with the president. The manager desperately wanted to avoid that problem in the future because he very much respected the president, who was an extraordinarily capable man. The university had prospered considerably during his fifteen-year tenure.

After exposure to the material in this book, the manager was able to analyze the president's actions vis-à-vis the trustees and discover a clear pattern which he did not originally see. The analysis showed that the president's job had a great deal of dependence associated with it. Predictably, the president spent considerable time trying to manage that dependence. Over a five-year period, his actions aimed at managing his relationship with the trustees included:

- Initiating a movement to increase the number of trustees from 15 to 45. The official rationale was that it allowed "more alumni participation in the university's decision-making process." It also, of course, made the president less dependent on any single trustee or small group of trustees, since two thirds of them had to agree before they could initiate anything important (like replacing the president).
- Initiating a change in the frequency with which trustees met, from monthly to quarterly. The official reason was that "our trustees are all busy and important people." This change made it virtually impossible for the trustees to really analyze or discuss any issues of importance and made them dependent on the university's staff work. Thus the president gained some important countervailing power.
- Establishing an office of the trustees, for "coordination purposes." He then made a school policy that all communication to the trustees go through the office, which was staffed by one full-time person who was appointed by the president. For all practical purposes, the president and his staff were able to control what information the trustees received, giving him more countervailing power.
- Recommending as possible new trustees people who did not live near the university ("we want the *best* people, regardless of where they now live") and whom he had favorable relations with. These actions resulted in the appointment of new trustees the president already had some power over, while making it more difficult than ever for the trustees to work together except through the quarterly luncheon.

One final thought in closing. Exposure to the material in this book can be especially useful for people who, from the point of view of a management career, have had "disadvantaged backgrounds." This includes those who have had little opportunity to assume positions of leadership and responsibility early in their careers, those whose formal education has not exposed them to issues of power and dependence, and those who have had little opportunity to interact with really outstanding managers. Such historical constraints do not have to doom people to lackluster careers. These people can be educated. They can nurture and develop their power skills, if they are aware of the patterns described in this book. Awareness is the first and the key step.

A woman in a middle management position wrote an informative letter in response to an article that contained much of the material in Chapters 2, 3, and 4.[1] She says the article brought new insight "just at the time when 'being a woman' no longer fully explained my difficulty in being considered effective or successful."

This manager continues: "Through ignorance of power and a close acquaintance with dependence, I have undermined my effectiveness in many small ways not related to results of performance. And because I don't want to coerce, manipulate, or boss, the drawback of using persuasion to influence someone who 'chooses not to listen or does not listen carefully' is part of my experience too. The light has dawned on some previously inexplicable promotions, game plans, decisions, and choices which, I see now, probably were attempts by management to manage relationships and control others in a very complex and dependent organizational environment."

She says that because of cultural bias against power and because of "women's social conditioning to be dependent and powerless," it is no wonder that "a large number of managers—especially the young, well-educated ones— perform significantly below their potential because they do not understand the dynamics of power and because they have not nurtured and developed the instincts needed to effectively acquire and use power."

She goes on to note that utilizing the methods used by successful managers "is possible for women, as well as for men. They don't require membership in 'the old boys' club' or having been raised to play team sports—just understanding and the desire to make them work for you. For once, I have no problem identifying with and emulating the characteristics listed of 'managers who are successful at acquiring considerable power and using it to manage their dependence on others.' "

She concluded: "Every example caused me to think of a situation or person in my professional experience to illustrate and bring home the point and, more important, to point out what I can do in my current environment to be more effective. That means that I can train myself to instinctively recognize the opportunities to acquire and use power as they occur. In many cases, I think I'm just a step away from doing the things that will make the difference."

8

Some recommendations

Power in management is a complex topic that does not reduce easily to simple "how to" prescriptions. Nevertheless, it would be in the best interest of most managers to follow these guidelines:

1. Identify your own power skills and abilities.

The first step in applying the ideas in this book is to examine your own behavior, especially in light of Chapters 3 and 4. Brutal honesty is needed here, and other people's perceptions can be most helpful. Use the following questions to focus your self-examination:

- Are you sensitive to where power exists in your organization? Or do you find yourself often surprised at how influential someone is, at key promotion decisions, or at someone's ability to block your initiative?
- Do you use all the methods described in Chapter 3 to develop power? If not, which do you tend to ignore? Why do you ignore them—because you simply have not been exposed to people who use them successfully or because you feel they are wrong?
- Do you take calculated risks with your power by investing it in

activities and decisions in the hopes of gaining even more power in return? Or do you tend to focus on jealously guarding the power you have?

- Are you sensitive to the power implications of all your actions? Or do you sometimes inadvertently make decisions or take actions that put you in a worse position?
- Has your career path thus far moved you toward key sources of power in your organization? Do you know where those key sources are?
- Are you sensitive to what others consider to be legitimate behavior in using power? Do you recognize that most people believe that power carries with it certain obligations regarding its use?
- Do you have a good intuitive understanding of the various ways managers use power? Or are you surprised by some of the statements in Figure 3?
- Do you use all the methods of influence mentioned in Chapter 4? If not, which do you tend to ignore? Why do you ignore them—because of a lack of familiarity or a feeling that they should not be used?
- Do you use your power to influence and manage all those people you are dependent upon? Or do you tend to concentrate more on one set, such as subordinates, peers, outsiders, or supervisors?
- Overall, do others see you as powerful? As influential? If not, why not?

Answering these questions is important for two reasons. First of all, the identification of a weakness or a blind spot is a major step in overcoming it and developing your skills. Second, knowing yourself well is a crucial requirement for making good career decisions.

2. *Explicitly take into account power and dependence when planning your career or seeking a job.*

If you have ideas about the type of job you want in two, five, ten, and twenty years, use Chapter 5 to help you identify how much those jobs are likely to make you dependent on others (Review Figure 6.) Then ask yourself a very important question: In light of your current power skills and abilities, is it likely that you will be able to cope effectively with the dependences inherent in those jobs? If the answer is no, you had better start reexamining your career goals.

If you have never explicitly identified the type of job you would like in the future, Chapters 5 and 7 can help you focus in on appropriate career paths. If, for example, you conclude that your power skills are weak and that you just cannot stand being highly dependent on a large number of people, you might consider focusing on staff specialist career paths in well-managed, moderate to small profit-making organizations.

Before seeking a specific job or accepting one, it would also be wise to do a more detailed power/dependence analysis, a few examples of which were given in Chapter 5. The analysis would involve identifying in some detail the dependence associated with a specific job you are interested in. From that, you can get a general idea of the type and amount of power-oriented behavior needed to cope effectively with the dependence in that job. With a corresponding knowledge of your own power skills and abilities, you can then reasonably predict how effective you will be in the job. In this way, you can avoid seeking or accepting an inappropriate job.

3. *Before starting a new job, carefully consider what sequence of activities can help you develop the power you will need.*

Managers seldom start a job with all the power they need to perform it effectively. That power must be developed. As we saw rather clearly in Chapter 2, in the example of Dave Hirsch and Jerry Donatur, the exact sequence of activities that one engages in on a new job can either help or seriously hinder the development of that power.

Here are three good rules of thumb for identifying an effective sequence of activities in a new job:

- Unless the situation is a crisis that demands immediate action, begin by spending considerable time developing relationships and gathering information.

- Take on any low-cost/high-payoff tasks first—that is, tasks that require little power to implement but have the possibility of yielding high returns in power.
- Never tackle a problem until you have more than enough power to implement a solution.

4. *If you are less effective at your current job than you desire, check to see if it is a power/dependence problem.*

Identify the people you are dependent upon. Be careful not to ignore anyone. Consider people above you, below you, in other departments, and outside your organization. Then diagnose how you are currently acquiring and using power to cope with each of those dependences. Have you developed sufficient countervailing power in all instances? Are you actively trying to manage each of these dependences?

Using this process you may find the sources of some of your current job ineffectiveness. And once identified, you should be able to take corrective action, much like the examples in Chapter 7.

In addition, whenever you are having specific problems dealing with, understanding, or influencing people, or with implementing some program, think about the situation from the point of view of power, dependence, and influence. Ask yourself:

- Who has what power in this situation, and who is dependent upon whom?
- How have recent events changed this situation?
- What effect would future alternatives that you or others are considering have on this situation?

Good answers to these questions can sometimes make a big difference in your effectiveness.

5. *If you find yourself in a job whose dependences are significantly greater than your power skills and you are unable to change the situation without misusing power, GET OUT!*

As we saw rather clearly in Chapter 6, a large gap between power skills and job-related dependence inevitably contributes to organizational ineffectiveness. If you do not effectively manage your job-related dependences, you will not fulfill your job responsibilities, or you will end up coping with the difficult situation by misusing power. (Figure 6 summarizes these ideas.) If you find yourself in such a situation, I hope you remember the stories of Walt Sofer, George Miller, and Ron Kaplan.

> 6. *Whenever you have the opportunity, try to influence educators and management development personnel to focus more on power and influence.*

A former student of mine, who was unaware of my recent work on power, wrote in 1977 to let me know how he was progressing in his career. He praised the school and the MBA program and offered only one criticism: "There should be more explicit consideration of the issues of power and politics within the corporate world. I understand that it is a sort of 'taboo' subject; besides it is very difficult to teach anything about it. But a more recurrent exposure to 'power dealing' cases, in a more apparent way, will, in my opinion, enhance the effectiveness of the program." I could not agree with him more.

The topic of power has been left out of management education for too long. If you have an opportunity to help change this, please do not pass it up.

Index